HER HOME

HER HOME

A Woman's Guide to Buying Real Estate

by
RUTH REJNIS

ANCHOR PRESS/DOUBLEDAY
GARDEN CITY, NEW YORK
1980

Library of Congress Cataloging in Publication Data
Rejnis, Ruth.
Her Home.
Includes index.
1. House buying—United States.
2. Single women—United States—Economic conditions.
I. Title.
HD1379.R45   643
ISBN: 0-385-13609-9
Library of Congress Catalog Card Number 79-7206

First Edition

BOOK DESIGN BY BENTE HAMANN

For my godmother,
Ruth A. Burns

2071863

Contents

1

Decisions, Decisions, Decisions

Should I buy a house or stay in my apartment? I may be wasting money by renting, but can I afford to buy? Will I be able to get a mortgage? Can I handle the upkeep of a house—what do I know about boilers and waste lines? I'd like to have my own home, though, and my accountant is telling me I need the tax deduction. I don't know . . . it's a big step.

It certainly is. A house is probably the biggest financial investment most of us ever make. But if you are reading this book, somewhere, perhaps very much in the back of your mind, is the thought that financially you can be doing better for yourself by owning instead of renting, and that is wise thinking. The purpose of this book is to assure you that if you have a regular income—and not necessarily a grand one—and a good credit record, you can probably buy a house. And you can maintain it, even if your father, the super, or your ex-husband has always made the repairs where you have lived before.

Real estate is probably the best investment you can make—

before diamonds, art, stocks, and certainly before letting any sizable chunk of money sit in a savings account, where your $1,000 will next year be worth $900. It is a safe investment and one that lies within the range of most pocketbooks. Stocks are risky, the art market fluctuates and sales cannot always be made when you would like, but real estate becomes increasingly important and valuable as the population and its demands grow. "Buy land," advised Will Rogers. "They're not making any more of it." And in a more romantic vein are the words of Gerald O'Hara to his daughter in *Gone With the Wind:* "Land is the only thing that matters, Katie Scarlett. It's the only thing that lasts." And we all knew how Ms. O'Hara felt about Tara. Real estate *is* an investment, of course, which always carries a degree of risk. But it is rare for anyone to lose money on a house, unless it has been left to wrack and ruin. Even then it will probably bring more than its purchase price twenty years ago, because of inflation. The land on which it stands may make it more valuable, too. Real estate is, quite simply, the simplest long-term way for most of us to keep inflation at bay.

Buying a home has always been a major step for any family —a serious decision, well thought out and entered into with excitement, trepidation, and the awesome feeling of Assuming One's Responsibilities. A woman buying a house by herself knows all of these emotions, plus, understandably, her own special worries about upkeep and "being in this all by myself." But it is happening all across the country. Young single women are buying ten-room houses in older city neighborhoods. Stately homes that once belonged to the gentry of the community and echoed with the noises of children now reverberate to the sounds of hammers and buzz saws. Thousands of women of all ages are purchasing condominiums and townhouses. Women nearing retirement, who may have lived for many years in houses, are coming up with ways of keeping their homes despite reduced incomes and growing maintenance expenses. They are creating a rental unit or two, or they are taking roommates. They see the wisdom, economic and otherwise, of keeping their homes.

Single people, male and female, have become a prime market for homeownership in the last half dozen years or so. A survey by the New York *Times* in more than a dozen key areas of the country found that single people of all ages were buying from 10 to 20 per cent of all homes purchased. That includes single buyers, unmarried couples, or adult males or females teaming up.

A study by Investors Mortgage Insurance Company (IMIC) of Boston, a leading private mortgage insurance organization, found "single women bought 1 out of every 14 homes sold in 1977—up from 1 in 16 in 1976." As you read this, that figure is expected to be 1 in 10.

Several developments have brought about this trend toward ownership. As women move up the career ladder and their incomes rise, they become more aware of the need to invest their money smartly. Qualified women are not being denied credit any longer, and that includes mortgage money. Passage of the Equal Credit Opportunity Act (ECOA) of 1975 had a lot to do with helping women become acceptable mortgage loan applicants. The act prohibits creditors from discriminating on the basis of sex or marital status in any aspect of a credit transaction. (In 1977, the act was extended to ban discrimination also on the basis of race, color, religion, age or national origin.)

The IMIC survey provided this picture of the female home buyer: Legal, medical, and accounting professionals were in the lead among house hunters. Teachers, then stewardesses, and then nurses headed other major career categories. The average age of the women was thirty-four. Almost four fifths were under forty-five years of age. In the early 1970s, when home buying was still new to women, the trend was toward two or more women teaming up to buy a house; in the late 1970s this was no longer the case—women were buying on their own, wanting privacy, and being able to afford it.

While single women—and "single" throughout this book

refers to women who have never been married, plus women who are widowed, separated, or divorced—have been purchasing all types of housing, it is the condominium that is responsible for easing most of them into ownership. Those units, small, manageable, and affordable, have attracted more female buyers than builders and marketing experts initially expected. In the early 1970s, to cite one example, a developer marketing condominium complexes in Denver and in a Chicago suburb aimed those units at the professional man. Model apartments were decorated to suggest that herein resides A Playboy. But of the first hundred buyers, ten were women. Not about to lose any potential market, the company redecorated and reslanted its advertising. This has happened in many new developments. Today, the single woman figures as prominently in advertising campaigns and marketing approaches for condominiums—and just about every other housing style, too—as the single man, the childless couple, and the retired "empty nester."

What type of women buy homes? Generally, they are more mature, though not necessarily older. They are career-oriented and are concerned about their finances. Says Meta, a real estate broker in New York's Westchester County, who has seen the number of single women home buyers double in that area within two years: "The typical buyer is in the professions. She is sensible and sophisticated." Female buyers are practical and know what they want, added another woman who sells real estate in the county, "but any first-time buyer needs a lot of stroking."

Is buying a house the right decision for every woman? If you think you might move to Houston within the year, better stay in an apartment. If you have a small income and many responsibilities—to aged parents, say—better not buy a house. If you're saving to buy a bar on the west coast of Ireland, homeownership may be a step in the wrong direction, unless the bar is many years down the road, in which case you may actually be saving money by owning and may make a nice little profit when you sell. If you live high on a modest salary—the best clothes and restaurants, Europe every year—you may find the cutting back that almost always comes with owning and maintaining a house too much of a sacrifice.

Otherwise, if you're twenty-six years old and earn $15,000 a year, you can afford a house. If you are sixty-two and find a traditional single-family home too large and expensive, there are other ownership styles you may not have considered that would suit perfectly. In fact, there is something for every taste and bankbook when it comes to housing.

Your decision isn't irreversible, either, which some first-time buyers do not take into account. If you don't like the house, or if you don't like owning *a* house, you can always sell, and usually make a profit while you are about it. The average American moves seven times in his or her lifetime, so unless you are ninety-two years old, this is not likely to be your last move. Don't spend too much time, either, thinking, "What if I get married?" "What if I change jobs?" "What if the hassles of the city get to me and I want to move to the mountains?" Planning for the future is wise—up to a point. But too many women never unpack their suitcases, figuratively speaking, waiting for the great "what-if." If the house doesn't suit you, one year or ten years after you move in, you sell it. Nothing is forever.

Most women buy their own homes because they want the space, privacy, and design a private home can afford. But a number buy only because it is the best decision for their financial future. Owning real estate is one of the best hedges against inflation. House resale prices are rising at an average annual rate of about 13 per cent, a little higher than the over-all inflation spiral. Homeowners enjoy tax benefits, which become particularly important to women as their incomes rise and the tax bite becomes heavier. Single women know all about high taxes. In fact, a financial adviser will usually tell a woman with a rising salary to buy a house before making any other investment. Mortgage interest and local property taxes on a house are tax deductible. In the early years of a mortgage, almost all of the mortgage payment is interest, which can be particularly beneficial come tax time.

There are other attractions to homeowning. "A man's home is his castle" is pretty accurate, no matter who owns the castle. In yours you can renovate and redecorate to your heart's content, with no landlord around to take the hammer out of your hand. If you want ten cats, you can have them. If you want a guest room instead of making do with a convertible sofa in the living room, you can have that too. There may be a yard where you can garden. You will make more friends among the folks living near you because the time spent talking to neighbors is worth the investment. They are not like the tenants down the hall who may be moving out in a few months' time. You will feel—in a challenging, not a musty way—that you have settled down.

Finally, there is that somewhat clichéd phrase "pride of ownership" that supposedly comes with the keys to a house. It *will* attack you at some point in those early days after you move into your three-room condominium, or seven-room Victorian, or seventeen-by-sixty-foot mobile home. As one young woman who has owned a house for two years laughingly put it, "I feel as if, well, I'm a grown-up now."

Somewhere in the thought process of most tenants who are considering the purchase of a home comes the question: Is it cheaper to rent or to buy?

In the short run, it is cheaper to rent. In the long run it is cheaper to buy, as you'll see.

On the side of renting, the news has been good. In the last five years, rents, on the average, have risen 26 per cent, while incomes have increased about 45 per cent.

The homeowner, meanwhile, has faced severely rising costs in that time period. According to the U. S. Departments of Labor, Commerce, and Housing and Urban Development (HUD), the cost of new homes in the five years prior to this writing has risen 57 per cent. A new home now costs over

$60,000. Fuel costs in general are up 65 per cent; property taxes, up 63 per cent, mortgage payments, up 74 per cent. All of these expenses have risen, and sharply, while the cost of renting has actually declined when compared to income. The homeowner is, of course, building up equity in his investment, which should become more valuable over the years, while the renter has nothing to show for his or her living expenses. Owning a home is still "the American dream" and most people do regard rent payments as money down the drain or merely an adequate style of living until there is the money to buy.

The home buyer faces a fixed mortgage expense for twenty or thirty years, while rents *will* rise. In fact, there has been a slowdown of rental construction in the last few years for a variety of reasons, and that will force rents up in existing buildings. A house is a good hedge against that spiral and against the over-all inflation rise. As dollars become cheaper, mortgage payments become easier to make with those cheaper dollars. During all of this, your income is continuing to rise, too.

It is a complicated picture that economists do not always agree upon. All say there are "hidden factors" to consider in the buy-versus-rent question. For example, where would the down payment for a house be invested otherwise?

Far more satisfying than having several successive landlords think you're a peach, however, is having your money working for *you*, not making someone else rich. You might think of it this way: At just a 10 per cent annual appreciation rate, a house costing $45,000 will increase in value by $4,500 the first year. That's $375 a month. If that home was purchased with a down payment of $10,000, in just a little over two years that initial investment would be recovered.

Renters sometimes reason that by not paying out mortgage, tax, and fuel costs, they can put their money to other uses. That has usually been found to be a fallacy. The only other use their money goes for is rent, or it sits in a savings account or is dribbled away in purchases hard to recall.

Just about everyone who has bought a home has said, "It's

the best investment I ever made." If you do decide to buy, don't wait. The time will never be better and prices will not be lower. Historically, the only time house prices have fallen very much has been during depressions, where there are very few who can or want to buy homes. As long as there is inflation, where the problem is to find a hedge against erosion in the value of a dollar, that does not happen.

If it can at all be worked into your future plans and present economic situation—buy. Enjoy living in your own home, and let your money start earning *you* money.

2

Financing
Your Purchase

Forget the old ethic about borrowing. Only four out of every hundred home buyers pay cash; the rest assume mortgages. So you are likely to have to go into debt to buy a house. But it will be the most constructive debt you will ever enter into—and you will have a lot of company!

The discussion of financing comes before house hunting because it is important to see your financial picture clearly *before* you start calling on real estate agents and making Sunday drives to see what is on the market. It is useless and defeating to look at houses that are beyond your means. Better to be armed beforehand with the knowledge of exactly what you can afford and the various ways in which a house can be financed. A real estate broker will explain financing procedures to you, of course, but that confusing array of terms and figures can more easily be digested first on your own. Also, *you* know more about your housing needs and financial capabilities than realty agents do, no matter how much information you feed them.

The old saw of buying a house that costs no more than two and a half times your annual income is still true, although some lending institutions will stretch that figure to three times.

Generally, though, if you are making $20,000 a year, it is assumed that you can afford a house with a price tag of $50,000. There is no use looking at $85,000 homes, because you will not be able to get a mortgage for one, unless possibly you are putting up a huge down payment. So with the cost of new houses now close to $70,000, that $20,000 income means that you will probably have to purchase an older house, which indeed most first-time buyers do. (New mobile homes can be purchased for $50,000 and well under that amount. They are considered in Chapter 6.)

Where is the money to come from? Even if you have a meager savings account, it is possible for you to own a house, thanks to the growing number of programs started in the last few years to bring homeownership within the range of lower-middle- and middle-income buyers, especially young, first-time buyers, who are usually stunned at the prices of homes and the down payments required. So the financing plans are there, and the houses are, too. Let's see how you can buy one.

PAYING CASH

It seems like the perfect deal if you can plunk down full cash payment for your house. As stated earlier, few can afford to do so, but it may not be wise to pay cash even if you have the money right under your mattress. There are these arguments for assuming a mortgage: You can pay off that fixed mortgage debt with inflation-cheapened dollars; the mortgage is a good, forced-savings program; the smaller your initial dollar investment, the larger the rate of return on your capital as your property goes up in value. If your paycheck keeps pace with today's double-digit inflation—at this writing about 12 per cent annually—in ten or fifteen years your mortgage dollar will be only half as large a share of your income as it is today. Everything will go up—prices, your income—but that mortgage payment.

One exception to all of the above might be a retired woman who may prefer to pay cash for a house rather than be burdened with mortgage payments. For everyone else, a mortgage will probably be required, whether they would choose to pay cash or not. But before you go shopping for one, you might look at your own credit record.

ESTABLISHING CREDIT

If you have never borrowed from a bank and have always paid cash for your clothing and other expenses—that is a sorry situation. Every woman should have a credit record. It will be difficult for you to secure a mortgage—the highest debt you are likely to incur—if the lending institution has no proof that you are able to repay a loan. How can you build a credit record? You can start by applying for a small loan—$1,000 is usually the lowest amount you can borrow—and forget that you do not need the money. Repay the loan promptly and in as short a term as the bank will allow. Buy something on a store's installment plan and pay that off quickly. Then you will have a "credit history." For more ways to improve your over-all credit picture if you live in New York, Chicago, Miami, Houston, Los Angeles, or San Francisco, stop in a branch of the Citibank for a copy of their forty-page booklet *Borrowing Basics for Women*, or write Citibank at 399 Park Avenue, New York, New York 10022.

The Equal Credit Opportunity Act of 1975 prohibited lenders from discriminating on the basis of sex or marital status. In 1977 the act, as noted in Chapter 1, extended that protection to race, color, religion, national origin, and age, whether all or part of the applicant's income is derived from any public assistance program or whether the applicant has in good faith exercised any right under the Consumer Credit Protection Act. Creditors must consider all sources of income, including alimony, child support and part-time earnings. If you are married, creditors cannot automatically discount your salary when determining whether you and your husband can afford a house. Not like the old days when frequently the working wife was asked if she were practicing birth control!

Unfortunately, a residue of discrimination still exists, especially for formerly married women. A charge plate in the name of Mrs. Richard Jones does a woman little good if Mr. Jones has flown and she is now on her own. Many of these women have no property or assets in their own names, which is not good. The federal government and private agencies have, in the last few years, begun massive educational campaigns for women, informing them of their credit rights. Too few women know what these rights are, and not all lenders and even real estate agents have grasped the scope of equal credit and fair-housing laws. HUD has no concrete figures on the alleged discrimination against women, but Donna E. Shalala, Assistant Secretary of HUD for Policy Development and Research, says "we have no reason to believe there has been a massive turnaround." The government has awarded nearly $1 million in grants to carry out this education process. The money has gone to groups such as the League of Women Voters, to conduct workshops for women whose husbands no longer support them, and the National Council of Negro Women, for similar seminars.

While lenders may sometimes drag their feet, they *are* aware that they are in the business of making loans, and with inflation and other economic factors, they must start taking female applicants seriously. Most of them are. No altruistic motives here; just banking sense.

THE DOWN PAYMENT

Even if you are the lender's dream applicant for a mortgage, you will still have to come up with a down payment that will range from 10 to 30 per cent of the purchase price of a house, and frequently 40 and even 50 per cent. At the lower percentage rates, if you are purchasing a home for $50,000, you will need from $5,000 to $15,000. (This is for conventional mortgages, which are the most common. Special programs, which usually carry lower down-payment requirements, are considered on succeeding pages.) You will need another 5 to 8 per cent of purchase price for closing, or settlement, costs, an amount that must be handed over at the time you take title to your new home. More about those charges later, too.

If you do not have money for the down payment in hand, you can cash in savings bonds or stocks, borrow on life insurance policies, or sell valuable possessions. If you have $7,000, say, and need another $3,000, it would be better if you could borrow that amount from a relative than painstakingly save up for the next two years. Housing prices can be expected to continue climbing and so will down-payment requirements. You may never catch up. One young man borrowed the entire down payment he needed—$10,000—from his credit union. Lenders are wary of your borrowing to make up the down payment on a house, however, and with an amount as large as $10,000, they might justifiably question a borrower's ability to repay that loan and carry a mortgage as well. That man's bank didn't question his loan, but yours might.

Chicago Title Insurance Company found in its family housing bureau survey that first-time buyers made a down payment of 12.45 per cent of the purchase price of their homes. Almost 80 per cent of those buyers made their down payment from savings and investments. On the average, it had taken the first-time buyer less than two and a half years to save up for the down payment.

It is preferable to make as small a down payment as you are allowed, rather than toss in as much as you can. It is better to take as much financing as is available. The smaller amount will leave you a reserve fund for future emergencies. But more important, the less you put down, the greater your return on your dollar investment when you sell. A small down payment will mean higher monthly payments over the life of the mortgage, but this is made up in the income tax deductions you are allowed, which really reduce the cost of the mortgage. There are some advantages to a high down payment—the lender may allow you an interest rate a fraction of a percentage point lower than the prevailing rate. And, of course, if you want to buy a house a lender would find too expensive for you to carry, a huge down payment would mean a lower, more affordable mortgage.

Private mortgage insurance can help the buyer over the hurdle of down payment. With this insurance, which guarantees the buyer a mortgage with a low interest rate, you can purchase a house for as little as 5 per cent down. This plan is aimed at young, first-time buyers who could have difficulty raising the thousands of dollars needed to put down on a home these days. For lending institutions the program means a homeowner's loan is guaranteed and all risks vanish as far as they are concerned. The Mortgage Guaranty Insurance Corporation, based in Chicago, with offices in thirty cities, is the nation's first and largest mortgage insurance company. In its twenty years of existence it has insured nearly 20 million home loans. There are other concerns in the field as well.

The insurance costs 1 per cent of the mortgage amount, payable at the closing, and a quarter of one per cent payable each year on the outstanding mortgage balance. These payments stop after from ten to twelve years when the loan will no longer need to be insured. So if you purchase a $45,000 house and put $10,000 down, you would have to bring a $350 mortgage insurance fee with you to the closing and pay a smaller amount for each of the remaining years.

Applicants for mortgage insurance are notified of their acceptance quickly, usually twenty-four hours after application, and the process is not nearly so drawn out as it is with loans backed by the Federal Housing Administration (FHA), Veterans Administration (VA), or Farmers Home Administration (FmHA). You can ask your real estate agent about private mortgage insurance or contact one of the companies direct.

Your real estate agent will be acquainted with all of the programs mentioned in this chapter, but it is better to know something about them yourself. Some are more trouble for realty people than others and consequently may be relegated to their back burners. You'll have to ask. Also, be free in talking about your financial situation to the agent. Do not merely swallow hard when told you must come up with a $25,000 down payment in your section of the state and walk away mum to do your own calculating. Ask the agent if he or she can help you raise that amount. There are regional plans and programs affiliated with large realty offices to help buyers come up with those enormous down payments. Agents have to help buyers or there is no business for them in today's expensive housing market.

GOING AFTER A MORTGAGE

Most house hunters look for a house, fall in love with one, absolutely have to have *that* one, then apply for a mortgage and frequently find they have gone over their heads in what they will be allowed to buy. Disappointment and wasted effort. Buy a house in an orderly manner. Before you approach a real estate agent, take a moment to drop into a bank, preferably one to which you might apply for a mortgage, and ask a mortgage loan officer a few questions. In what price range should you be looking with your income? What is the bank's current interest rate and down-payment requirements? The loan officer cannot, of course, guarantee that your application would be approved, but at least you will have some idea if you are even inside the ballpark vis-à-vis house hunting.

Many lenders feel that mortgage payments and property taxes should not take more than 25 per cent of a borrower's annual income. Others say a borrower's mortgage, taxes, home insurance, and other long-term debts cannot exceed 30 per cent of their annual income. Once you know the lender's general requirements, you can sit down with a notebook and pen and figure your own indebtedness and how much house you can afford. Renting an apartment works differently, if you are thinking of house hunting in that context. There, you can go in a little deeper for an apartment you really like and cut back on other expenditures. But a bank looks at the hard, cold figures and will not allow you to extend yourself beyond what it thinks you can bear.

Some points to consider during that session with the notebook: What is the total of all your debts right now? Are you still making car payments, which can take a sizable chunk of your monthly income? If you have to borrow part of the down payment on the house, will you be able to handle that in addition to your new homeowner expenses?

What is your over-all worth? Consider insurance policies, annual wages as well as income from regular outside work, income from stocks, pensions, alimony, and other sources. Do you have any valuable possessions—jewels, antiques, art, and the like? One advantage to figuring your worth is that you will probably be pleasantly surprised at just how much that is.

You can get a mortgage if your income is, say, a relatively modest $14,000. But if, for example, you are a photographer employed by a magazine at that salary and are expecting to leave to become a full-time free lance, buy the house before you quit. Free lancers buy homes, of course, but being on someone's payroll still makes lenders feel more secure. Buy the house, therefore, before making a job switch that will pay you less or before leaving a company where you've been for several years. It all looks better on the mortgage application.

In some instances you may be required to have a cosigner on your mortgage application. Doreen, an automobile salesperson, did, as you will see in Chapter 4, about condominiums. Doreen needed a cosigner when she purchased a condo because her income was in commissions and her length of employment at the Ford dealership was only about a year.

Moving into a house brings special expenses during the first year—and all the other years, but as with a few of life's other endeavors, the first year is the hardest—and you should have cash reserves after the closing to meet those expenses. You will, for example, have to purchase garbage cans, shovels, perhaps a lawn mower. There will be frequent, and expensive, trips to the hardware store for widgets and gizmos you had not known existed. It costs a fair amount just getting set up. And that's not including unexpected crises with plumbers and roofers and tree surgeons. So leave yourself with *some* spending money after you take title to your house.

The following table shows what you will be expected to pay out monthly on a $40,000 mortgage if you buy a $50,000 house, with $10,000 down:

INTEREST RATE	LENGTH OF MORTGAGE			
	25 years	*30 years*	*35 years*	*40 years*
9%	$335.68	$321.85	$313.60	$308.55
9¼%	342.56	329.08	321.10	316.27
9½%	349.48	336.35	328.65	324.03
9¾%	356.46	343.67	336.24	331.83
10%	363.49	351.03	343.87	339.66
10¼%	370.56	358.45	351.55	347.53
10½%	377.68	365.90	359.26	355.43
10¾%	384.84	373.40	367.01	363.36
11%	392.05	380.93	374.79	371.32

Source: FINANCIAL PUBLISHING COMPANY

If you have done further calculating, you will have seen that, for example, the $50,000 house with a 9 per cent mortgage rate over twenty-five years will have cost a total of $100,704. If the same house carries a 11 per cent mortgage for twenty-five years it will have cost the buyer a total of $117,615. Shopping around for the best possible mortgage terms can therefore mean a saving of several thousand dollars over the life of the loan.

The monthly mortgage payments in the table comprise only principal and interest and do not include real estate taxes.

Most lenders will require that you make a payment to them of one twelfth of your annual property taxes each month along with your mortgage payment, and they make the realty tax payments for you. So if you have a 9 per cent mortgage for twenty-five years with a monthly payment of $335.68 and your property taxes are $2,400 a year, your payment each month to the bank will be $535.68.

Now that you have a general idea of what you can afford, you can think about finding the financing for that house. Mortgages can be obtained from several sources: savings banks, pension funds, savings and loan associations, commercial banks, insurance companies, and sometimes the seller of the house. As you have seen, it pays to shop around for the most favorable terms. Just because you have done all your banking in the bank near your office or in the neighborhood where you now live, it does not necessarily mean either bank should get your mortgage business. A bank around the corner or on the other side of town may offer better terms. Each lender has its own policy. Here, for example, are the requirements the *Jersey Journal* found for six banks in Jersey City, New Jersey.

BANK A   40 per cent of purchase price required as down payment for thirty-year mortgages, but customer must have had at least $10,000 on deposit at Bank A for more than a year.

BANK B   25–30 per cent down payment for Bank B depositors only.

BANK C   40 per cent down payment on 20–30-year mortgages.

BANK D   25 per cent down payments on twenty-five-year mortgages at 10½ per cent interest.

BANK E   25 per cent down payment only for depositors with accounts in bank for more than one year.

BANK F   25 per cent down payment on fifteen-year mort-
                gages that can be called in after five years or
                where the bank can increase the interest rate
                after five years.

Pretty harsh, aren't they? The nation's older cities have cautious lenders. If you live elsewhere, terms should be a little
easier. But not much. If you know it is likely that you will be
applying for a mortgage from a certain institution, deposit all
your money there right now, even if you expect house hunting
to take a year. When mortgage money gets tight, banks will
take care of their customers first. If your parents have said
they would give you $5,000 toward a down payment, take it
now, not when you are ready to apply for a mortgage, and deposit it with that lender.

Lending rates are high and are expected to continue rising.
The average life of a mortgage is twenty-five to thirty years,
but this too can vary.

What kind of mortgage will you get? A conventional mortgage is most common. That is where the buyer obtains from a
lending institution a twenty-five- or thirty-year loan at the prevailing interest rate. But there are variations on that simple
transaction, some of which are new programs that have been
introduced to bring homeownership to more middle- and
lower-middle-income buyers. Here then are other ways of
financing a home besides the clear-cut, conventional mortgage.

SELLER'S MORTGAGE

A growing number of sellers are providing mortgages for
buyers. More and more you will see in classified advertisements that sellers are willing to finance all or part of the
purchase of their homes. This is good for sellers if they do not
need the purchase price immediately, in that they can spread
out taxation of any capital gains resulting from that sale and

have a nice income on a timetable they arrange themselves. Seller financing is especially popular in neighborhoods where mortgage money has been difficult to find. There are many variations of this plan. Sometimes sellers will set terms of five years or so, until the buyer can obtain permanent financing. Other times the terms are like those of a lending institution: twenty-five- or thirty-year loans. It is especially important that both seller and buyer have legal counsel for this type of transaction, and that means attorneys knowledgeable in real estate and/or tax law, to see that minimum protection is afforded both parties. It is a complicated business and should not be undertaken by the two parties on their own.

FHA-, VA-, AND FmHA-BACKED LOANS

Loans backed by the FHA and the VA are not mortgages given by the government, a common misconception. Rather, they are guarantees undertaken by the two federal agencies that make the mortgage more attractive to lenders since payment will be made by the agencies if you default. Both types of "loans," as they are usually called, erroneously or not, offer the most generous terms around, including no down payment required for qualifying veterans. (Widows of veterans who have died of a service-connected disability also qualify for VA loans if they have not since remarried.) The FHA requires down payments of 3 per cent of the first $25,000 of a loan, 5 per cent of the amount above $25,000. The highest mortgage for a single-family home the FHA will insure as of 1979 is $60,000. The interest rate is usually a fraction of a per cent point below the prevailing rate. Buyers of any income qualify for FHA-insured mortgages. VA-insured loans can run as high as the appraisal value of the house.

In both loans, buyers can be charged no more than one "point"—a bank's service charge for processing the loan. (Not all mortgage loans incur points charges.) A point equals 1 per cent of the amount of the mortgage.

Real estate agents and lenders do not like to deal with these loans because of the enormous paperwork and lengthy processing time involved. Sellers do not like the loans because the properties must meet the agencies' long set of minimum standards of habitability. It is not uncommon for agencies to refuse a loan unless the seller fixes a leaky roof or sodden basement. Sometimes sellers are also charged "points" that would have been paid by the buyer in conventional financing. FHA- or VA-backed loans can take four weeks or more for approval. This can be exasperating for the buyer and for the seller, who technically has his property off the market during that time without knowing whether it has been sold.

You do not have to be a farmer to qualify for loans insured by the FmHA, but you must live in a community with a population of 10,000 or under (in some rare instances, 20,000 or under is acceptable), and you must be unable to obtain a mortgage from a private lender to buy, build, or even renovate a house. FmHA loans carry no down-payment requirements and can take thirty-three years to repay. Interest rates are usually only a bit below the prevailing rate, but can, in hardship cases, be as low as 1 per cent. You cannot buy that vacation cabin in the woods under this program—only year-round homes of no more than 1,300 square feet are eligible. This is a program for lower-income buyers with incomes under $16,000 a year (better check on this when you investigate the program —the income limit varies according to family members). There are no points charged these buyers.

In July 1978 the Justice Department announced that the FmHA had agreed to eliminate what a civil rights official had called an "alarming" bias against women buying into the FmHA programs. Apparently the regulations contained numerous references to "the borrower's wife," "the farmer's wife," and the like. An FmHA task force was assigned to rewrite the farm home loan regulations to make women feel more welcome.

CREDIT UNION MORTGAGES

The nation's 12,600 federally chartered credit unions began offering thirty-year mortgage loans in May 1978. Prior to that, credit unions had been allowed to make loans for only ten or twelve years, although some state-chartered unions had been granting longer terms. Credit unions in general are groups of persons with something in common—education, employment, religion, etc.—so if you are not already a credit union member, you might look around for one to join. Because credit unions are tax exempt and officers serve voluntarily, they have few costs and can pay more interest on savings and charge lower rates on loans than other lenders.

URBAN HOMESTEADING

You read all about urban homesteading when local governments began early in the 1970s to sell or offer through a lottery vacant city properties they acquired through transfer from HUD. The houses, many of them tumbledown shells, were sold for token sums, sometimes as little as $1.00 to individuals or families who would make repairs to meet minimum standards before moving in. Then, within eighteen months of living in the house, they would bring it up to local code standards. When the homesteader had done that and had lived in the house for at least three years, he or she received full title to the property. If the house cost only $1.00, then the only regular outlay of cash the owner would have to make from then on would be for real estate taxes, water, and sewerage. There are now thirty-nine cities with HUD homesteading programs. For women with low incomes and with several children needing the space of a house, homesteading can offer perhaps their only way to homeownership. Several women in those circumstances have taken that step and are delighted with their new homes.

Fine, you say, I buy a shell for $1.00. Where is the money to come from for renovation? Most of those thirty-nine cities also offer low-cost rehabilitation loans of close to $40,000 per house, with interest ranging from 1 to 7 per cent and the terms of the loan running from twenty to thirty years. The size of the family and the applicant's income are taken into account. Repaying the loan could be the same as, or close to, the amount you are paying for rent right now. For more information about urban homesteading, contact the HUD office in your area.

NEIGHBORHOOD LOAN PROGRAM

The neighborhood loan program (NLP) is a state-sponsored plan to spur homeownership in the cities. It provides an 8 per cent mortgage, with down payment requirements ranging from zero to 10 per cent. FHA and VA loan guarantees are accepted. The loans are available for so-called redlined sections of certain city neighborhoods. That is where banks allegedly refuse to grant mortgage money or make those loans prohibitively high for fear, they claim, of losing their investment in sections of the city where property values have been declining. Yes, some of those neighborhoods are pretty bad. But some are not. And as more and more cities "come back" with the growing return of the middle class, some very attractive houses indeed can be found in those mapped sections.

With minor differences from one region to another, the loans are available on one- to four-family owner-occupied homes. There is no income limit for buyers, but the credit standards are the same as for conventional loans, and granting the mortgage commitment is left to the discretion of the lender. The maximum allowed for a single-family dwelling is now $45,000. The program can be used for financing new residential construction, but its primary purpose is to aid existing housing in "underserviced" neighborhoods.

The neighborhoods eligible for the NLP are chosen in consultation with municipal officials. They have to be basically stable and primarily residential, areas where decay and blight have not reached too advanced a stage and where financing has been difficult.

The semiautonomous state agencies that direct this program make the mortgage money available through the sale of bonds. When they have the financial commitment, they go to banks in the state to draw up a list of those who will participate as lenders. When you buy a house and apply for a NLP mortgage, the agency buys your mortgage from that lender. But you send your mortgage payment directly to the bank each month, just as you would with a conventional mortgage.

Contact the community affairs department in your state capital for more information about this program and for maps of the eligible blocks in the city in which you are interested. This is another excellent opportunity for women with low to moderate incomes and little available for a down payment to purchase a house.

In general, it is a good idea to check with your local HUD office or your city's community development agency when you are thinking of buying a house. They may have regional programs to help moderate-income buyers, and they may have corresponding low-interest-rate home improvement loan programs, for fixing up those houses once you buy.

SOME NEW PROGRAMS

As the cost of buying houses has risen beyond the pocketbooks of most first-time buyers, economists, bankers, and government officials have been forced to come up with programs to ease those folks into ownership. What have developed over the last several years are several innovative programs. They are new, they are not available nationwide, and there is still some skepticism about their worth. But *you* may be able to buy a house with one of them.

Variable rate mortgages (VRMs) are in use at savings and loan associations in about a dozen states. The VRM is usually offered at half a percentage point below the going interest rate, but after five years it fluctuates, depending on such factors as the long-term federal bond rate. When the key indicators, whichever ones are used, rise, interest on your mortgage goes up, and when they go down, so does the interest. So the initial payments for your mortgage are set, but you will not know how those terms will change over the life of the loan. You are betting that interest rates will go down, but will they? The program is too new for any indication of its saving to the buyer.

Although the interest will fluctuate over the years, lenders have set up maximums for that percentage, and for the life of the loan that rate can go up no more than 2.5 per cent.

VRMs have not exactly taken off as fast as a Concorde, perhaps because there is little impact made on monthly mortgage payments with them and perhaps because of the cynical disbelief of young, first-time buyers, toward whom it is directed, that mortgage rates, or the cost of anything else for that matter, will ever come down. There is no going back to their parents' good old days of 5 per cent mortgages, and that is where the difference would be appreciable.

Graduated payment mortgages (GPMs) are new, too, and were also created for the young house hunter. Here payments rise as the homeowner gets older, on the theory that his or her income will be rising as well. Graduated payment mortgages come in government-insured, privately-insured, and uninsured programs. If you buy a home for $100,000 and make a down payment of $40,000 and assume a $60,000 mortgage at 9 per cent over thirty years, you would start out with a monthly payment of $365. Each year your monthly payment increases until you are paying $524 a month in the sixth year. The table stabilizes then and the payments remain the same for the balance of the loan. If you had a conventional loan for that amount, you would pay $483 each month for the entire thirty years. Over-all, the GPM interest charges would be higher.

The peril in obtaining a GPM, of course, lies in your assumption that your income will rise. It *probably* will, and only you can determine if gambling on such a mortgage is any gamble at all.

CLOSING COSTS

Two to four months will elapse from the time you put a binder on a house until you are actually handed the keys to your new home. During that time your mortgage application will be reviewed and approved, the house will be appraised by the lender, the title search will be made to assure that there are no claims on the property, and a near ton of paperwork will be moved back and forth, much of it requiring your signature. Then a date will be set for "closing." Your lawyer will notify you, and the seller will also be alerted. On that auspicious day the seller and the buyer, their counsel, and the real estate agent meet to transfer ownership. It is a solemn ceremony in that thousands of dollars change hands and you the buyer become progressively poorer as your signature is called for on various disbursements of your money. Settlement costs run from 5 to 8 per cent of the purchase price of the house and *must* be paid at the closing. What you are paying for is the mortgage application fee, the appraisal fee, your attorney's fee ($300–500), title search, title insurance, survey and recording fees. You will also have to pay one year's homeowner insurance fee and deposit in escrow real estate taxes for a certain period before your monthly mortgage-interest-taxes joint payment picks up that charge. Any points you will be charged are payable here, too.

Lenders have been under fire in recent years as homeowners complain of escalating settlement costs and the fact that they are unprepared for those charges on the day of closing. Settlements come under the Real Estate Settlement Procedures Act (RESPA), which is intended to provide advance knowledge of costs, reduce the amount homebuyers have to place in escrow accounts for real estate and insurance payments, and do away with kickbacks and referral fees. RESPA requires that mortgage loan applicants receive a special information booklet describing settlement practices and costs. Still, HUD is considering revisions to those rules, as settlement costs still rankle homeowners.

Generally, a month or so before closing the bank granting you a mortgage will send you a printed form filled in with your estimated closing costs, although the bottom of that sheet may say something like "This form does not cover all items you will be required to pay in cash at settlement. You may wish to inquire as to the amounts of such other items you may be required to pay at settlement." By all means, call the lender to determine those extra costs, if in your case there will be any. You are entitled to a full disclosure statement. You cannot be expected to go into a closing not knowing what it is going to cost you. Your lender should also have available for you a copy of the booklet *Settlement Costs and You; a HUD Guide for Home Buyers*.

MORTGAGE PREPAYMENT

Some lenders will not let you prepay without your forfeiting all or part of the interest you would have paid over the entire course of the loan. No cancellation of the interest charge, in other words. Other lenders will not allow you to prepay during the first few years of a mortgage. It is advantageous to have the option to prepay. But should you? If you are a typical middle-income first-time buyer the question is academic. Where would you get the money to pay off a mortgage now? But let's say you come into an inheritance or win a lottery. You might be tempted to pay off that mortgage debt. If you are the type that fritters money away, it might be a good idea to prepay if you can before the cash just disappears. You will have greater equity in your home—a considerable savings. Prepayment might also make sense for women who are at or nearing retirement and who do not want to bother with the burden of a mortgage. Check your lender if you ever find yourself in a position where you would like to pay off all or part of your mortgage to see what penalties will be exacted and what you can be expected to gain.

Now that you have a clearer picture of how much you can spend for a home and where that money is likely to come from, you can contact a real estate agent and go shopping for that most important purchase of your life—a house.

FOR MORE INFORMATION:

The Superintendent of Documents, U. S. Government Printing Office, Washington, D.C. 20402, offers the following publications:

Rent or Buy? 80 cents. 32 pages. 1974.

Selecting and Financing a Home. $1.10. 23 pages. 1977.

Wise Home Buying. Free. 28 pages. 1978.

Settlement Costs. $1.00. 40 pages. 1978.

3

Going House Hunting

Now that you know where the money for a house is likely to come from, you can start looking—a hunt that may take a year or longer. Or perhaps you will find just what you want immediately. It happens. But before scattering your efforts like buckshot, looking at townhouses and then farms and then ranch homes and perhaps a loft, narrow yourself down at least to whether you will want the city, suburbia, or exurbia. The chapters on condominiums, cooperatives, and mobile homes offer more insight into those housing styles. This one will concern itself with the traditional single-family home. There is plenty to think about when preparing yourself for *that* purchase.

City v. Suburbs
No doubt you know where you will end up buying, although that may not be the area you would prefer. What the city has going for it are its well-touted cultural advantages, ease of transportation, and houses less expensive than those in surrounding "bedroom communities." Many urban homes offer

huge amounts of space and the careful workmanship that will
never come our way again.

A number of houses you will be looking at will be in what
are now "revival" neighborhoods, which are being occupied by
a growing number of middle-income professionals who are re-
storing both the homes and the communities. Don't be put off
by a few rundown houses in a neighborhood—that does not
necessarily mean blight has hit. But most houses should look
cared for. In many revival enclaves there is a small community
association composed of residents dedicated to the renaissance
or continued maintenance of the neighborhood. These people
are good to talk to when you are house hunting. They can steer
you to houses for sale, introduce you to prospective neighbors,
aid you, at least in spirit, in your restoration efforts, and guide
you to lenders who are amenable to mortgages in that area.

One problem with city houses is the mortgage. Some sections of town, perhaps the one you are interested in, are
redlined. That is not to say buyers do not obtain mortgages in
less desirable sections of town, but rather that they have to do
more shopping around for mortgages than they had planned.
If this happens to you, the real estate agent can help. So can
that community organization.

When it comes to culture, the suburbs are no longer a desert, but many singles and single parents still prefer an urban
environment. The "Noah's Ark" syndrome still prevails in
suburbia. But those communities do have space, greenery,
quiet, and other attributes that make for good living. If a suburban town is your choice, do primarily consider your commutation costs if your job is in the city. They can be sizable—$50,
$60, $70 a month. If there is no public transportation and you
do not have a car, can you afford to buy and maintain one?

City or suburbs—this is the time to bring out and dust off all
those old dreams about the kind of house you always wanted.
No doubt there was no price tag on that dream house, but
even now, with a budget, you may be able to find one or two
of those features you always thought would come along with

the house you bought. A bay window, a sun porch, a small garden—there are $35,000 houses with those features. In Chapter
7, "Housing Choices for Special Times of Your Life," there is
advice to divorced, widowed, and retired women that they
should like at least *one* aspect of their new housing style, no
matter how many concessions they will otherwise have to
make to finances, family, geography, etc. The same is true for
any home buyer. Don't just buy a house because it is the closest
one to the grammar school or across the street from a bus stop.
Love at least one room or design feature—you are paying a lot
for this property and perhaps will be there for many years.
You're entitled.

Even if you are planning to buy a year from now, it cannot
hurt to start going to open houses now. They are listed in the
real estate classified advertisements of newspapers and are an
excellent way of seeing how much some homes are costing and
what buyers are getting for their money. Since this is not
serious house hunting, visit $200,000 homes, even if you are
planning to spend $55,000. Another interesting aspect of mak-
ing the open-house circuit is that there are always real estate
agents on duty at these homes, and during a slow period when
there is little traffic, they can answer your questions about
prices in that neighborhood, housing prices in general, taxes,
and any other aspect of ownership. The agents will have no
telephone interruptions and will give you their undivided attention.

House tours are another way of seeing how other people live
and are great fun, too. Go whenever you see a tour announced
in a neighborhood you might be interested in buying into. The
fee is small—$2.00 to $4.00—and you can visit seven to ten
homes, taking all day if you wish. In restored or renovated city
homes especially, owners are not the least bit shy of telling vis-
itors how much they paid for the house, what the taxes are,
what it cost to have the floors scraped, or whatever. They will
give you the names of good local workmen and maybe detailed
instructions on how you can expose a brick wall, landscape the

yard the way they have, and find that shade of green paint you've been looking for. These are people, city or suburbs, who are proud of their homes and their communities. They have the enthusiasm and patience to answer endless questions about either.

Your Job

You have already considered commutation costs vis-à-vis a suburban or city house, but there are other aspects of your work to think through as well.

If you plan to do a lot of work at home or to operate entirely from the house you buy, naturally every property you inspect should be assessed as a potential office as well as home. By judiciously shopping around, Cecily, for instance, managed to find exactly what she was looking for to provide both living space and room for her photography business. It is a house with a large living room that doubles as a studio, lots of light in the kitchen to set up photo equipment, two bedrooms and bath on the first floor, where her models can change clothes, and three bedrooms upstairs.

Check storage space if your work will require that or if you refinish furniture or have tons of sports equipment or are engaged in any sport or work that comes with a lot of gear.

If you are planning to buy a house and then open a boutique or hairdressing place on the ground floor, be sure to investigate whether that block is zoned for commercial use before you buy the house. To find it zoned as strictly residential could put a devastating crimp in your plans, unless you apply for a zoning variance which you may or may not win.

Even if you do not work at home now, if you have a talent that could, no matter how far in the future, develop into a paying business, you might keep that in the back of your mind when you are house hunting. Study all the rooms to see if any would lend themselves to conversion to a serious work area. If you are into catering, can the kitchen accommodate restaurant stoves? If you are collecting antiques with the thought of opening a shop one day, consider where you can store what you are buying now. For dressmaker, artist, sculptor—whatever your creative bent—certain homes will work better than others when you decide to combine living and working space.

Maybe a Loft?

Perhaps you can work better in the spacious, light-filled space of a loft. "Alternative uses of existing buildings" is an expression that cropped up over the last few years. It may be the rundown factory turned into a chic collection of shops, the unused railroad station transformed into a restaurant, and now, the recycling of loft space into living quarters. (A loft building, incidentally, is defined as a structure of more than one story, which was built for storage, manufacturing, or some other commercial use.)

The growing popularity of lofts has meant, for one thing, that they are not as inexpensive as they once were. As high-income professionals move in, doing elaborate renovations and forcing prices up, the lower-income groups are finding there is no room for them. If you live in a large city, where there are many loft buildings, you may still be able to find a bargain, perhaps in an out-of-the-way locale that has not yet been "discovered."

The principal problem with lofts is that many of them are being used illegally by residents. One half of New York City lofts, for example, are lived in illegally. This means the building does not have the needed zoning variance for residential use or it does not come up to building code standards and thus has no "Certificate of Occupancy," a designation needed for legal residential use.

If you want to purchase a loft in a building not legally qualified for living in, and then plunk down an enormous sum of money to renovate the space—which sometimes means installing heat, plumbing, bathrooms, new floors, and the like—

you will have plenty of company in which to have anxiety attacks over your illegal status. Needless to say, it would be much better to find a building that will spare you all that grief.

A good book that will conduct the reader through the labyrinthine maze of zoning laws, housing codes, building inspectors, and the like is *Pioneering in the Urban Wilderness: All About Lofts* by Jim Stratton. Urizen Books, 66 West Broadway, New York, New York 10007, is the publisher. The price was $7.95 in 1977 when the book was published. Stratton covers loft living in twenty-four major cities, although most of his information was garnered from his own renovation of three lofts in Manhattan's SoHo, where most of that city's loft transformations are taking place.

Your Family

The needs and desires of those with whom you live will also enter into your decision of which house to buy. If you are a single parent, your children will probably be the overriding consideration—"whatever is best for the children." You will consider the schools, bus transportation to school, and the safety of the community. If you are moving to an older street, where perhaps there are many couples whose children are grown, how far will your children have to go to find playmates? If the kids are in or near their teens, how are they going to get around if they have no car? Hauling and carting youngsters about makes many parents opt for the city over the suburbs.

How about your parents and other family members? If you think you may have an aged relative living with you in the next few years, try to buy space accordingly. Or if you cannot afford to buy a large house this time, keep in mind a potential division of the ones you can afford when going through them. You can always move again when a parent comes to live with you, but if you can plan ahead with this purchase, you'll save yourself another exhausting, potentially expensive search for another house.

A Rental Income

There is a back-to-the-city trend nowadays that is seeing many shoppers, particularly single people, select townhouses. Many of these dwellings are row houses, featuring ten to twenty rooms, naturally far too large for today's small families. Some are rooming houses. If these homes interest you, you might consider taking a floor-through or duplex apartment in one of them and converting the remaining space to one or more rental units. This can be an excellent investment and help defray your living costs at the same time.

It is especially important that that type of property is in good condition. As a landlord, you will not want the phone ringing off the hook with complaints about malfunctioning or nonfunctioning plumbing, electricity, or heating. A house inspection is a must here prior to purchase. More about them later. 2071863

Another point to consider when looking at these houses is, if they are now single-family, whether you can convert them according to existing zoning laws. And what are you supposed to do if four tenants or nine roomers come with the property? Laws vary. Sometimes you can evict unwanted tenants when you move in; sometimes tenants come with the lawn and garage. It is an unpleasant situation and can sometimes be downright sad. The problem of urban dislocation—when middle-income buyers move into a previously low-income neighborhood, renovating houses and moving prices and rents up, thereby forcing initial residents out—is perhaps the most serious one in the back-to-the-city movement. Truly responsible homeowners, sensitive to the needs of the community, may not want to turn out low-income families, but on the other hand they may need every last penny of that increased rent money. Housing specialists are still trying to find a solution to that quagmire that would satisfy both income groups. So if you buy an apartment or rooming house, better find out your legal status as a landlord.

Becoming a fledgling entrepreneur by managing a house with one or two or more rental units is the first step many small investors take. More about this in Chapter 10, about investing. For the moment, it should merely be noted before you buy the house that you will probably earn every penny you make as a landlord. If owning a house makes you less free than you were as an apartment tenant, becoming a landlord in that house ties you down even more. You will be almost always on call and cannot leave for extended trips without making arrangements for the care of the house should an emergency arise. Repair bills can mount up and so can just plain maintenance. The rents can pay the mortgage, taxes, and, if you are lucky, some additional expenses. All that is certainly nothing to sniff at. But there is still the expense—to be absorbed by you—of plumbing bills, repainting the hallways, replacing the roof, and so on.

However, many homeowners swear by the appearance of that rent check or two every month: makes it all worthwhile. Most of those who buy these properties consider them an investment, though. They do not expect to come out ahead on the monthly rents. If they net a few dollars, great. But operating expenses frequently eat up the rent payments.

Some women, when they buy this type of property, become handy and do many of these jobs themselves. Others are not interested and prefer to earn enough money to pay someone else to do them. Married women who buy and renovate old houses do have it easier than single women in one regard. It *is* nice to have a man around the house—to shut off the water when a pipe bursts, to carry heavy lumber, to intimidate surly workmen. Sometimes coping alone with all that gets to single women (and to single men, too, no doubt). Some get through the first few rough years and then sail merrily on. Others cave in. Sari, who is divorced and in her forties, purchased a house with a small garden apartment suitable for a single occupant. She kept the upstairs duplex. She went through an unlucky stream of tenants in the first four years of ownership. But that has not bothered her as much as the costs of repairs and how difficult it is to find people to make them. On her income as a free-lance illustrator, she was particularly frightened every time a damp patch appeared on a ceiling or the latest water bill rolled in. She finally has thrown her hands up and is seriously considering moving to a high-rise apartment in a nearby community with her mother, who is moving back North from Florida. One gets tired of coping.

Repair men (and it is still usually men) are very often extra courteous to women alone and indeed frequently adopt a chivalrous attitude. But a few rip them off, too. Wherever possible, it is a good idea to have a male friend or relative around the day you are getting estimates on a large job to be done, even if that man is merely sitting at the table reading a newspaper.

But some women manage beautifully when it comes to repairs, even though they were thirty-three years old before they saw a Phillips screwdriver. You will probably be able to do more than you think, and you will understand more of how things work than you imagine. There is no reason to know *every* intricacy of heating and plumbing units, just as there is no need to be able to take a car apart and put it back together again to be a competent driver. You can learn just enough to know how to fix what you can and when to call in help.

You can snake a sink drain, change fuses, clear downspouts, and of course, do all but the most difficult painting. Some women will even do that. You can expose a brick wall, which is not difficult. And there are many women, with no previous training or even interest, who have installed tile, tarred a roof, put down carpeting, and changed electrical fixtures. Whether you enjoy doing it or cannot afford to farm it out, you will be surprised at your talents!

There is no need to be afraid of living in a house by yourself or of keeping it up. The house has stood there for thirty, fifty, or one hundred fifty years without falling down; whatever assaults you make on it are not likely to cause too much damage. If you are truly worried about your ability to manage a single-family house, there is always the excellent alternative of purchasing a condominium or cooperative. It *is* true that in a traditional house there is always something that needs to be done or something that has just broken. And always on a Sunday morning.

Finally, in general, no matter how much you like a house, always look at it with an eye toward its resale value. Anything a little offbeat may become an albatross when you decide to sell. A five-bedroom house may be difficult to find a buyer for and so may a one-bedroom in some locations. Those who are frequently transferred by their employers know to buy the most ordinary of homes because they sell quickly when the orders for the next move come through. That does not mean you should do without interesting features—a loft bedroom, a skylight, a greenhouse—that may, in fact, enhance the value of the home. But there are some features that attract more buyers than others. A pool, for example, will attract a smaller number of potential buyers than a house without one; some people worry about small children falling in. A tennis court is a plus. In Connecticut, there is a revolving house that rotates one complete turn every twenty-four hours. It was designed by the architect-owner, who recently spent two or three years trying to sell it. No doubt he expected that wait, but three years is a long time if you are in a hurry to move. *Moral:* Whatever you buy should appeal to the greatest number of potential buyers, unless you are prepared to sit a while when you decide to sell.

To get an accurate idea of what the house you are interested in is going to cost you in running expenses, the real estate agent can tell you the annual property taxes, but it is a good idea to ask the owner to show you a few typical fuel bills, so that expense is not needlessly eye-opening once you move in. Ask what the water/sewerage bills are for the year. And the cost of a commutation ticket.

If you are buying a house that needs a good deal of work, be aware now of what you are letting yourself in for. If you will have to have the work done in stages, as you can afford to pay for it, be sure you can stand living in a "work-in-progress" for a year or two or even three. This is an enormous job you are undertaking. *Know* you will be inhaling plaster dust for a good long while. Those who have been through remodeling an entire house say it is wise to finish one room quickly. You can head there when despair sets in and admire what the house will ultimately look like. It's a good room to have when relatives show up, too. They can see that there is hope for the house after all.

IF YOU BUY WITH SOMEONE ELSE

If you are married, you will probably buy a house under what is technically called "joint tenancy with right of survivorship." This is the most common shared-property arrangement for married couples, although more than two buyers can be involved. Under this style of ownership, each person owns an equal share of the property. When one owner dies, his or her share passes immediately to the survivor, with no delay while the will is being probated. (This arrangement is no substitute for having a will, however.)

The other popular shared-property ownership style is "tenants in common." Here, the disposition of your share of the property after your death is according to instructions in your will. This style is common if you buy a house with friends or strangers who may not inherit your share. The lawyer you engage to buy a house can help you on ownership questions and how best to word documents if you are buying with someone to whom you are not married.

Friends are buying houses together these days, and so are strangers. With the steady waning of the traditional "nuclear family" and the rise of single, divorced, and separated persons and childless couples, large houses would frequently sit vacant if these people did not join together to buy them.

Most of these new "families" find an excellent housing buy, where zoning laws work in their favor.

Jo and Howard are both single, in their thirties, and on the faculty at a state college in an older urban city in the East. Although the two lead unrelated lives, with separate friends, they have something else in common: a brooding, four-story brownstone they purchased together. They bought the house as tenants in common, although they have designated certain areas for separate use.

"We worked together on committees and we assumed we could run a house the same way," Jo explained. "Besides, this was the only way either of us was going to get a house."

There are several reasons why unrelated persons are sharing houses. Those old large houses are more affordable than new or nearly new ones. According to a recent U. S. Census Bureau report, for the first time in history the average American household consists of fewer than three persons. So those rambling homesteads that once housed an "extended family" are simply too large for today's buyers. A fourteen-room house can, however, be split into two comfortable seven-room units. Finally, with landlord-tenant relations frequently unpleasant and with rent controls keeping a lid on profits to be realized from rental units, many owners of large houses are reluctant to turn unused rooms into apartments and take on the headaches of renting. Better to find someone to share the whole house.

Jo could have afforded a house, but after looking at a sound-but-in-need-of-work brownstone in her city, she was dismayed. "I told Howard, 'It's too big. It scares me.'" Howard wouldn't have minded the work, but he could not afford to buy a house. "Then," Jo continued, "one of us said, 'Want to share it?' It seems incredible, but we didn't discuss details until after we bought it." It should be added here that there is no romance involved, Jo explains. She and Howard are just co-workers and friends.

The house cost $29,000. A mortgage was secured locally

with no trouble, as was a $20,000 renovation loan. Mortgage, taxes, loan payment, and utility bills are paid each month from the couple's joint checking account marked "house funds." Howard chips in a little more, as prescribed, since Jo paid more of the down payment. At a certain point, when Howard has paid enough in, they will be even.

The house is interestingly divided. Neither wanted the first two floors, so the garden level is rented, with the income going into the house fund. Howard lives on the top floor, Jo on the second. And the two rooms on the first, or parlor, floor have been transformed into a formal joint reception/dining area, which they put to good use with large family dinners and joint civic and school meetings.

A lawyer drew up the contract for the couple, outlining the disposition of the property in the event of a sale by either party, death, or default. As most such contracts do, it gave the remaining party the option of purchasing the other's share or approval of the new owner.

Although the mundane details of running their house could also have been set in print, Jo and Howard have worked them out informally. She, for example, looked into insurance, he contacted the utilities. Both of them deal with contractors and keep up the common areas. "I feel if we try to formalize it too much we're going to blow the whole thing," said Jo.

For Nancy and John the business of being landlords in their Manhattan townhouse had already soured when, conveniently, both their troublesome tenants moved out. This time the couple decided to sell the other half of the house—two floors. They went to the first couple who replied to their small newspaper advertisement. Nancy said the selling price of the other part of the house was based on the market value of the whole building, the size of the two existing mortgages, and the cost of renovation. Very complicated to work out, she said, but both sides are satisfied.

If you are interested in a situation similar to one of the above, both of you should agree on how you want to live in that house: Go all out and renovate it or make only minimum improvements? Buy the best in construction and decorating materials, buy anything for now, or wait until you can afford top quality? Estimate as carefully as possible the costs of running the property and, finally, to avoid arguments, install separate meters for electricity, and possibly heat, in each unit.

All sharers make this one admission. Early in the relationship one party took the other aside and politely complained about an uneven division of work. But adjustments were made and things have run smoothly since. Said one sharer: "For some reason, when you get a $1,000 roofing bill and you know it's going to be split in half, it doesn't hurt as much."

THE REAL ESTATE AGENT

Rather than merely driving around the neighborhood that interests you looking for FOR SALE signs, register with one, or a few, real estate agents. While they all probably subscribe to a Multiple Listing Service (MLS) that circulates information about the same houses up for sale among many brokers, each office also has its own exclusive listings. Or you may be called about the house before it hits the MLS circuit. So registering with more than one office is not a duplication of effort. Deal only with full-time salespersons or brokers; no part-timers.

If you are buying in a "hot" neighborhood, where demand is high, call agents once a week to keep your name in front of their minds. Register with many agencies, and even try to meet some folks in that community, perhaps through their community association. They may know of houses coming up for sale, and you will get an early tip.

Realty agents are there to make a sale and expect to urge concessions on both buyers and sellers. But remember, they are working for the seller of the house in which you are interested and are trying to get the best price for the seller. You can, by the way, make any offer for a house, no matter how low it is, as long as it isn't ridiculously so. An agent is required by law to present all serious offers to the seller. Offering $20,000 for a house listed at $60,000 is not considered a serious offer. But $45,000 would be. Or even $43,000. If it's in a sorry state, go even lower. If you want the house and can only offer far less than the asking price, make your offer anyhow. If they come back to ask you to raise your offer, you'll know they are interested—that buyers are not exactly waiting in line for that house. When you offer more money, do so in $100 increments, not $500 ones. Go up v-e-r-y slowly. It is a war of nerves, but if you keep yours steady, you may win your house. If you absolutely have to have that house and can afford to go higher in price, you may decide that losing it is too high a price to pay for being clever. That's up to you. In any event, you can bargain over price as you would in a Moroccan bazaar.

Although the preceding chapter told you how much you should expect to pay for a house, given your income and other obligations, you will look at higher-priced homes anyway. Sometimes it is just for fun, but perhaps you will find yourself making a serious offer for one. Still, if you plan to pay $55,000, you can expect finally to buy a house for about $58,000. Most buyers do end up with something a few thousand dollars over their budget.

Be honest and open with the realty agent about the price range of houses you can afford. Agents usually do not ask your income, assuming that whatever price you tell them is what you can afford. You are either a $50,000, a $150,000 customer, or one where the sky's the limit. No matter what you tell them, they may throw in a few higher-priced models to show you— after all, their commission (generally 6 per cent of the sale price) on that sale would be higher—but for the most part they will follow your directives.

Ask if the realty agency can spare a copy of a typical mortgage calculation book, which shows how much you would have to pay each month for an X dollar mortgage at an X per cent interest rate. These booklets are hard to come by for the general public, but can be most helpful during your house hunting days. If there are no extras, ask if someone can make Xerox copies of the few pages that would be applicable to your situation. A bookstore with a comprehensive selection of real estate/financial books may have a slim paperback called "Monthly Amortized Mortgage Payments" or something similar. Coles Publishing Company, an international house with no offices in this country, publishes a book with just that title for under $2.50. Your bookstore might carry it.

LOOKING OVER A HOUSE

There are probably hundreds of points to consider when looking seriously at a house, from its appearance as you drive toward it to whether there are termites secretly gnawing away at the foundation of the back porch. You can't expect to learn everything about a house by walking through it—each has its own particular quirks—but you can pick up enough to avoid making the costly mistake of buying one in miserable shape (unless you know exactly what is wrong and how much it will cost you to fix it). The purchase price should reflect the seller's concession to the house's flaws.

House Inspection

It is a very good idea to have the house you would like to buy looked over by someone from a house inspection service or an engineer familiar with that type of structure. House inspection services charge varying rates, from $75 to $200 or more, depending on the comprehensiveness of their examination. They can be found in the Yellow Pages, but better check the local Better Business Bureau if you are hiring a concern unknown to you to see if any complaints have been filed against it. It might be even wiser to ask friends whom they would recommend or call a community or block association. Sometimes it has a list of workmen its members speak highly of. If you are buying a tumbledown hundred-year-old house that will need much repair, try not to hire a suburban service that deals almost exclusively with fifteen-year-old ranch homes. That old house needs the attention of someone who knows the eccentricities of elderly buildings and the fact that some of them will never be 100 per cent perfect.

There is no need to have a house inspector look at every house you are interested in before you make an offer. When you sign a contract for the house you finally select, one of the qualifications usually written into that document is that purchase is contingent on the report of an engineer or inspection service that is satisfactory to you. If that is not in the printed contract you are presented with, by all means have it written in.

What You Can Check Yourself

As you walk through the house, look to see if suitable building materials were used throughout. Walls should be checked for cracks that in newer construction indicate poor construction. (Don't worry too much about this in very old houses. Settling occurs and frequently there are cracks. If some cracks are bad, you may have to consider a major plastering job, however.) Are the floors level and free of squeaks? Do the windows close tight? Check for insulation around windows and in the basement and attic. Do screens and storm windows come with the house? If not, and insulation is poor, you may have to spend a few thousand dollars to purchase them. Look at the number of electrical outlets in each room to see if they are sufficient. Make sure the water pressure is good by turning on several faucets at once.

While in the basement, look at beams and supports. Any sags could mean the whole structure is shaky. Is the basement dry? Does it smell damp, musty, and is there evidence of rust? Are there high-water marks along the wall? A wet basement is a major source of grief to homeowners. What about the pipes? Copper, bronze, and brass are best. You can check for termites,

but it is a complicated procedure and a house inspection service or exterminator can do a better job. Have it done—it's
worth the price. An infestation can be costly, not to mention
damaging to the house. How is the house heated? As noted
earlier you should feel free to ask the seller to show you some
fuel bills.

What about water? Is the house connected to the city water
main or to a well? Is it connected to a sewerage system or a
septic tank on the property? How often does the tank need
cleaning and what does that cost?

Make sure you know what appliances or furnishings go with
the house—room air conditioners, awnings, etc. What goes
with the sale should be listed in the realty agent's book. But
some items are negotiable. If you bargain over price and you
raise your offer a few hundred dollars, you might also ask that,
say, the carpeting or shutters or whatever be included in the
sale. All verbal agreements should be followed up in writing,
in this case in the eventual sales contract.

It is not likely that you will go up and inspect the roof, but
an engineer or house inspector will.

It is a rare house that is thoroughly up to date in the energy-
efficient area. Still, you can count on a row house having lower
energy costs, all things considered, than a detached one. A
basement is more energy-efficient than a crawl space.

Homeowners' Warranty

A growing number of new homes are protected by a warranty. The National Association of Home Builders sponsors
one of the largest programs. Their HomeOwners' Warranty
program (HOW) lasts ten years, and the warranty stays with
the house if it changes hands during that time. The builder
bears the cost of the warranty, which runs about $2.00 per
$1,000 of the selling price of the house. The builder's guaran-
tees to the buyer are heavy during the first two years of the life
of the house—protection against defects in workmanship, materials, and structure and a pledge that the plumbing, heating,

cooling, and electrical systems will perform satisfactorily. In the last eight years of its life, the warranty covers "major structural defects," and that phrase, as might be expected, is frequently open to interpretation. What the homeowner and what the builder consider "major" can differ. But there is a HOW council that arbitrates disputes. The warranty is passed on to you at the closing of the house.

Only 11 per cent of the houses built in 1978 were covered by the program. It obviously could be more aggressively sold to builders.

UNFAIR HOUSING PRACTICES

Discrimination still exists, which will come as no great news to those of you who have felt its sting. You are not likely to be the victim of it because you are a woman—banks and realty agents are bending over backward for fear of having suits brought against them these days—but on racial, religious, and ethnic grounds, yes, there can be problems. Not always. Many house hunters sail right through, buying the house of their choice. Some find roadblocks.

The Civil Rights Act of 1968 made it illegal to discriminate in housing because of race, color, creed, or national origin. Since then HUD has conducted many surveys to check on that enforcement. The most recent survey took six hundred men and women and paired them by age, sex, dress, income, and marital status. They were so schooled that to any real estate agent the only difference between them as applicants would be that some couples were white and others black. Initial results of that survey showed that if black buyers go to four real estate agencies, there is a 62 per cent chance of their encountering discrimination. That discrimination can work in several ways. In some instances, black applicants are not shown houses until their credit ratings are checked, while the white applicants are immediately driven off to look at homes. Sometimes financing is different for each, with percentage points higher for blacks. More commonly the sin is one of omission—the black applicant is just not shown homes in certain communities and is directed to other, designated, towns. "Racial steering" it is called.

If you are savvy about the housing stock in the community in which you are interested and know that you want to look at whatever you jolly well want to look at, you can return home after a discouraging day of house hunting and call your local HUD office to charge discrimination. Or call HUD's toll free number: 800-424-8590. The agency will take it from there. If the worst happens, you will be involved in a court case, but if discrimination can be proved, you will have the right to buy that house. Other agencies that should be contacted are your local human or civil rights commission in your state government offices, the National Urban League, the National Association for the Advancement of Colored People (NAACP), and the American Civil Liberties Union (ACLU). But if you have to choose one, call HUD. It has the toughest laws.

Is it worth it to fight? That is for you to decide. But the laws are there and they cannot be enforced if those who are discriminated against do not come forth. There is a principle involved here. By your silence you give encouragement to bias and weaken the nation's fair housing laws.

WHEN YOU FIND THE HOUSE YOU WANT

Finally. You have found a house for which you would like to make an offer to purchase. Your offer is accepted. Then what? You will probably be asked to sign a sales contract or agreement and make a deposit, usually of 10 per cent of the purchase price. The agreement will set the sale price, the amount of the down payment, how the sale will be financed, your right to have a house inspection service or an engineer look at the property, and the delivery of a clear title. If certain extra items in the house—draperies, carpeting, etc., are to be included in the sale, they are listed. The contract should also provide for the return of your deposit if those conditions are not met.

It is wise to have a lawyer represent you in the purchase of a house. The lawyer will, for one thing, look over that contract for you. The fee is only about 1 per cent of the purchase price of the house and worth it. Most of the documents presented to you were drawn up to favor the seller.

You are usually entitled to return to the house just before the closing for one final look to see that no drastic changes have taken place in the two or three months between the acceptance of your offer and settlement. If you would like to see the house in that interim period, to measure for draperies, say, better have that visit included in the contract. Sellers may not be amenable to future visits, aside from the final one they must allow you, once the contract has been signed.

Sometime before the date of the closing ceremony—when the house changes hands and becomes yours—the realty agent will notify you that you will need homeowner's insurance. In fact the mortgage will be issued contingent upon your purchasing such coverage. Frequently the real estate office also sells insurance, and they will quite naturally offer to provide the coverage you need. Nothing wrong with that, although you may save a little by shopping around first.

The most common policy—and do check the variations in the event one of them would be more use to you than others—is called a "homeowner's policy" and covers the house, garage, and other structures on the property. Your personal property—household contents, clothing, etc.—is included, whether their loss occurs on the premises or off. If your home cannot be occupied because of fire or water damage, hotel and restaurant bills are covered, too. There is also liability coverage for any family members who live at home. How large a policy should you purchase? You should buy insurance covering at least 80 per cent of the value of the house *as it is today*, if you cannot afford total replacement coverage.

Details regarding the closing ceremony were contained at the end of the previous chapter on financing. This chapter has concerned itself with the traditional single-family home. The next three consider some alternatives to that housing style: the condominium, the cooperative, and the mobile home.

4

Mondo Condo . . .

The word rolls easily over the tongue now. No stammering or halting and starting over. *Condominium.* To the especially au courant it is "condo." As the word settles into the vocabulary, the style of housing it represents becomes more familiar in the landscape, in classified advertisements, and in daily life.

Women have been especially attracted to condominiums, principally because, while they offer ownership, it is of a reasonably small and manageable space, not a sprawling house. Since it is almost always attached housing, the condominium also offers more security than a suburban house on a quarter acre of land would. In high-rise condominiums there is usually lobby security personnel and electronic devices, and even in garden communities there is at the very least the closeness of one's neighbors. Complexes catering to young single buyers usually offer an active social program, of course, but in any condominium community there is the opportunity to make close friends, which does not always present itself that readily in other ownership styles, or, of course, apartment rentals.

The explosive construction of these jointly owned apartment

units began more than fifteen years ago. Although a few problems remain to be worked out, condominiums have settled in nicely as a unique form of homeownership. A style more complicated than others, but one that, if properly run, should bring no more headaches than usually go along with living *anywhere,* as owner or tenant. The condominium is definitely not a flash in the pan. Recent advances contributing to its growing stability are:

▪ An over-all healthier market. From a low point in 1975, it has rebounded nicely in both new construction starts and conversions from rental status.

▪ The rising cost of single-family homes, making the condominium the only affordable ownership style for many families. The average cost of new homes across the country is now (1979) close to $70,000. Condominiums suitable for small families can be purchases for $10,000 (and more) less than that price.

▪ Continuing legislation protecting the condominium buyer. Federal and state laws are continually being enacted. In Washington, the Community Associations Institute, composed of hundreds of community associations nationwide, is also keeping a watch on the rights of the purchaser and the regulation of the condominium community.

So, the construction of condominium developments should continue, although, given the ebbs and flows of the economy, some months and years, of course, will see more units built than others. Developers like condominiums because they utilize less land than a single-family development would and there is more profit in selling them. Buyers flocking to new developments, some indicated by no more than a sales trailer plunked in front of acres of muddy land, appear equally enraptured. They feel they are getting the best of both the homeowner's and tenant's worlds. Since a condominium buyer owns her apartment outright, plus a share of common facilities and areas in the complex, she is building equity rather than a drawer full of rent receipts. There are tax advantages to ownership, and elaborate remodeling and decorating can be done without bringing down the landlord's wrath. The size of the condominium is perfect for the growing number of single buyers, too.

No condominium owner will ever be found shoveling snow or patching a leaky roof—or hiring someone else to do it. The community association to which she belongs takes care of those bothersome and sometimes worrisome chores that go along with ownership of a single-family home. "It's a lazy man's house," said one satisfied owner. Ownership does not bring total euphoria, of course, but just as there are those who like apartment living and those who will head for the country, there will now probably always be those who will choose a condo, whether they want it in the city or in the suburbs or at the shore.

Joint ownership can come in many different styles, but basically there are two forms most prominent under the huge condominium umbrella. A strict condominium building is usually a high-rise in which owners (occupants) hold the title only to the interior space within their units. They have a percentage interest in the common elements: hallways, grounds, recreation facilities. The association to which the owners belong, and in which they also have a percentage interest, is the administrative vehicle for managing the commonly owned portions of the development.

The second style is the townhouse community or planned unit development (PUD). It is a fee-simple ownership wherein buyers hold title to their houses and the lots on which they stand. Usually, but not always, they provide their own maintenance. The commonly used property—walkways, a clubhouse, whatever—is owned by the development's nonprofit association in which homeowners are required to be members, but they do not own shares in that association or those facilities. It's more like a club they must join.

For purposes of uniformity in this chapter, the word "condominium" will be used to designate these and other ownership styles.

WHO IS BUYING CONDOMINIUMS?

Among those who buy condos are, first, those who cannot afford to buy a single-family home, a housing stock that has been rapidly priced out of the market for many Americans in the last few years, what with the high cost of new homes, mortgage rates over 10 per cent and still climbing, and down payments frequently as high as 40 per cent. The condominium is less expensive, and in new complexes the builder frequently requires down payments as low as 10 per cent.

Married couples without children account for a large number of buyers, and single house hunters are coming up fast as the market that many developers are courting.

Couples whose children are grown (euphemistically termed "empty nesters") often seek out "adult communities" run condominium style, where the age limits of unit owners are fixed—usually one must be forty-five or fifty years old or more to buy in—and children under eighteen years of age are not permitted as full-time residents. Besides offering less space to care for than private homes, condominiums ease the transition into apartment living for older people, many of whom are used to years of homeowning.

Finally, vacationers are buying condominiums in resort areas, for fun and, they hope, profit. Time-sharing, another form of condominium ownership, has also received much publicity in the last few years. More about that later.

Part of the attraction of condos is that buyers feel they are getting more for their money than single-family homeowners. In many shiny new complexes (and that's most of them) there are swimming pools, clubhouses, tennis courts, a marina, and a lively social program. Condominium dwellers appear to be spending their days in a resort hotel in high season. How can a middle-income, single-family homeowner hope to live like that?

These Xanadus are not without their drawbacks, naturally. A condominium is still an apartment, really, and that means togetherness living. Residents must follow rules laid down by the association running the project. There are the normal irritations of apartment living. Dr. Carl Norcross in his report *Townhouses and Condominiums: Residents' Likes and Dislikes*, published by the Urban Land Institute in Washington in 1973, surveyed 1,803 residents in forty-nine projects in Maryland, Virginia, and California and found the most common complaints to be, in descending order: living too close together; noisy neighbors (and especially noisy children); neighbors' dogs; subletters or renters of unsold units; inadequate parking spaces; the owners' association; poor construction; and dishonest salesmen.

Resale is another point a prospective owner should consider. Some units have been resold to a second owner, but in many complexes it is still too early to determine resale patterns—i.e., profit and how much of a profit.

Background of the Movement

The word "condominium" is Latin for joint ownership or control. And, although it may be the housing of the future, the style actually dates back to ancient Rome, where condominiums were employed to help solve that city's housing crisis. Desirable land, particularly in or close to the city, was as scarce in Roman days as it is everywhere today. To house Rome's swelling population the Senate passed a law that would allow Romans to own houses in multiunit dwellings.

Condominiums were also popular in the walled cities of the Middle Ages in Western Europe, until walled cities became obsolete and the population was permitted to scatter over the countryside where land was plentiful. From then on, that form of housing declined in usefulness and did not reappear in

Europe until the first half of the twentieth century, when the populous countries of Italy, Spain, Germany, Belgium, and France enacted statutes permitting condominiums. At the same time, England, although it did not enact the same legislation, began establishing condominium "flats."

Next the concept spread to Latin America and finally, in the 1940s, it reached the United States. Condominiums were not legal in this country, however, until 1951, when the Territory (now Commonwealth) of Puerto Rico passed a law establishing the legal status of the condominium to ease its own housing shortage. That law was further tightened in 1958 by the passage of the Horizontal Property Act, which governed the ownership of real property under the condominium method.

The concept then spread to the rest of the United States. In 1961 the United States Congress amended the National Housing Act to extend government insurance of mortgages to condominiums. This insurance was provided by the FHA, which is now part of HUD. The FHA, as noted in Chapter 2, does not lend mortgage money, but it insures loans made by private lenders for the construction, rehabilitation, and purchase of single or multifamily housing for rent or ownership. Although most housing loans in this country are "conventional"—that is, not insured by the government—FHA policies usually serve as guidelines for conventional lenders. In 1962, for instance, the FHA drew up a condominum statute based on the ones enacted by Puerto Rico. It subsequently served as a model for the rest of the United States in enacting condominium legislation.

By 1968 all fifty states had enacted laws making it easier to construct condominium complexes or purchase units in them, and the laws are still being strengthened, especially in the area of the rights of purchasers and of resident tenants in a condominium conversion. The rulings vary from one state to another, but they carry certain common elements:

- Recognition of joint ownership of all land and other areas within the boundaries of the structures that are not described as units.

- Establishment of a contract between co-owners that cannot be voided or altered without their joint consent.

- Separate taxation or taxation of the units individually and taxation of the purchaser's share of the common elements of the development on the basis of its value in relation to that of the other units.

BUYING A CONDOMINIUM

The purchase of a condominium is a little more complex than for a private home, but it is not an impenetrable maze. The following is an explanation of the principal points of ownership that will interest a prospective buyer.

Offering Plan

The "offering plan" is the booklet—sometimes running to 200 pages!—that tells the prospective buyer exactly what he or she is buying. It contains the name and address of the developer, floor plans of all apartments, the purchase price of apartments, the procedure to purchase, and page after page—frequently in legalese—outlining all other aspects of how the condominium will be sold and run. This is a complicated document about which you are sure to have questions. Ask them all. Most home buyers engage a lawyer to represent them at the closing of the transaction; if your lawyer is up on real estate law, so much the better for you on the complexities of the condo. Note two points, though: somewhere in the offering plan it will state that the plan has been filed with the state Department of State or Office of the Attorney General or whatever state office. This does not mean that that office has *approved* the developer's plan; it merely means that in some states that plan must be filed with the state. Also, if you engage the developer's lawyer throughout the sale transaction, remember that, fair as he may be, he is the *developer's* attorney.

Mortgage

One of the most important differences between cooperative and condominium forms of ownership is in financing. Securing a mortgage on a cooperative (see Chapter 5) can still be ticklish because a buyer owns stock in the *corporation* that entitles him or her to live in the unit. In the co-op the corporation actually owns the apartments, and some bankers do not want the difficulty of repossession (a rare happening anyway) because of the complicated ownership structure. But the condominium buyer, since she owns the unit outright, gets a deed that qualifies as collateral for a home mortgage. Mortgages for condos are usually obtainable from any bank or lending institution, just as they are for the private home buyer.

Mortgage terms vary according to the use of the condominium. A year-round home may qualify for a twenty-five- to thirty-year mortgage, with the usual down payment requirement asked of the single-family home buyer, although developers of some new complexes require down payments as low as 10 per cent. Mortgage interest rates are also the same as they are for the single-family homeowner. Vacation-home mortgages are treated a little differently. Here most banks will allow financing for only ten years or so on a unit that will not be the owner's principal residence.

As for women and condominium mortgages, all is well. In fact, condominium developers were gladly seeing that financing was arranged for the female buyer when women were still finding it difficult to purchase a single-family home.

Not of mortgage concern, but in the area of ownership, older buyers of condos should watch out for what is called "life estate" buying terms, if they are not fully aware of the restrictions of that style sometimes found in adult communities. It means you are buying the use of the property during your lifetime only. Upon your death, all your rights cease, and the townhouse or condominium unit becomes the property of the company that sold it, without payment. The company can then resell it to someone else. Buyers in adult communities should read their contracts carefully for mention of this practice.

Closing or Settlement Costs

When you purchase your unit you will be required to pay a mortgage service charge, a fee for transfer of ownership in resold condos, insurance, and other monies that will run between $1,000 and $2,000.

Utilities

Unit owners pay their own heat, gas, electricity, and air-conditioning charges, just as they would in a single-family home. An exception might be in a high-rise building with a common heating or air-conditioning unit where charges would be prorated among owners.

Property taxes

Real estate taxes are also assessed on the individual unit and are paid directly to the municipality by the apartment unit owner.

Maintenance Charges

You will be required to pay a percentage of common estate costs of the condominium complex each month. These include costs for water, sewerage, garbage disposal, and the upkeep of the grounds (grass cutting, snow removal, exterior painting). Not having to bother with those tasks is one of the attractions of condominium living, especially if you are planning to use your apartment only part of the year and do not want to worry about upkeep while you're away.

Maintenance charges can run from about $30 to $1,000 or more, depending on the size of the unit, its location within the complex, and even in what part of the country it is situated. Do these charges go up? They sure do and that is a frequent gripe of owners. But as costs rise, so must maintenance fees.

Although your mortgage check is sent directly to a bank or other lending institution, the maintenance check, sometimes referred to as "rent," goes to the association running the complex.

Tax Advantages

As an owner whose principal residence is the condominium, you are entitled to federal income tax deductions comparable to those of a private homeowner for expenses incurred in maintaining your property. First, the interest paid on the mortgage is deductible. So are the real estate taxes, plus any other taxes or assessments made against the property.

Selling Your Unit

You are, of course, free to sell your condo to anyone you choose and at any time you wish. Some condominium associations, however, hold the right of first refusal. That means you must present the name of the buyer to the association, and if it chooses, it can match the buyer's offer. The contract clause was set up to protect the condominium from undesirable commercial interests getting a toehold in the community and changing its character. The use of this clause is dwindling these days, presumably because there is no need to be overconcerned about such drastic changes within the community.

Much has been written about buying condominiums, but little is said about selling them. Although they have been established for some fifteen years, no definitive studies have been made on sales patterns. "The buildings are relatively new," said an officer of one builders' association, "and the newness hasn't put that many 'used' condos on the market. The people who bought them are, for the most part, still in them."

So, will you make a profit when you decide to sell your condominium? Well . . .

On the whole, sellers are finding that their condominium units are bringing prices that, all things being equal, are as good as, or higher than, those of single-family homes. But the prices depend on the same variables: location, appearance, convenience to shops, transportation, and schools, quality of construction and so on. The special concerns of buyers are how the entire complex is run, what its financial picture looks like, whether maintenance costs have been spiraling and whether there have been—or are likely to be—assessments on the complex pro rated among unit owners. Will buyers prefer the new condo to the older complex down the road? Again, no hard facts available. But an oceanfront or marina complex, no matter how many years old, will frequently have a waiting list while a new development but with less appeal will wait for buyers. Adult communities sell well, as a rule, and so do those that have won architectural awards and those that are in good downtown locations. One thing is certain, though: the buyer of several years ago was better off than today's condominium shopper when it comes to price. Just like everything else, new condominium communities are going up in price. One example: an award-winning marina complex about five miles from Manhattan. In 1976 a two-bedroom duplex apartment could be purchased there for $50,000. Construction is still going on and in today's market the selling price for a unit of that size is now $80,000. This is happening all across the country, of course. So if you're planning to buy, do it now.

WHO RUNS THE CONDOMINIUM COMPLEXES?

All condominium complexes, again using the term generically, have common facilities—grounds, lobbies, and so forth. These are administered by a community association which everyone is required to join by terms of the purchase agreement. Becoming a member assures you a vote in the decisions of the complex and guarantees the association your proportional share in the charges that go along with running the project. At the head of the association is an elected board of managers usually consisting of five, seven, or nine members. The project developer initially sets up the association and the voting rights that come with it. These are automatically transferred from the developer to the owners after a certain percentage of the units is sold. Voting power is usually based on a ratio of the purchase price to the total price of the project but sometimes on the floor area ratios.

In developments of under fifty or sixty units, the community association may directly handle services, repairs, and bill payments, but in larger complexes an outside firm is usually engaged to manage day-to-day operations.

Once settled in your condominium, take an active interest in the association running the complex. Former rental tenants may find this difficult. They are used to letting someone else worry about faulty plumbing and landscaping. But it's a different ballgame for the owner. An apartment it may be, but you have a deed to it and it's yours (and the bank's). The community association is making decisions about property in which you have equity.

GOOD AND BAD POINTS

All the condominium regulations seem neat and well structured in print. But how do they work? After all, the condominium buyer has a somewhat unique relationship with his or her fellow unit owners. The family that lives in a single-family house may be friendly with their neighbors or not. Rental apartment dwellers either ignore fellow tenants or join with them in the common bond of animosity toward the landlord. But condominium residents, since their ownership of the very lawn in front of their unit is shared with everyone else in the complex, must develop, if not friendship, at least a smooth working relationship with others in the complex and a total awareness of what's going on.

In general, problems in condominium communities fall into four areas:

▪ Construction defects.

▪ Budgets. Some people don't care how much is spent and others have to watch every $10.

▪ Lack of qualified property managers to run the community for the owners.

▪ Builders' reluctance to "open" their books to homeowners until they have to, which sometimes leads to immediate higher monthly costs because the builders absorbed so many expenses themselves to make the project appealing to buyers. Also, builders do not involve residents often enough in the running of the complex in its early stages, a conditioning process that many residents feel should begin at the time of the sale.

There are also initial bugs that have to be worked out in the relationship of unit owners among themselves, a few of which linger on long after the grass is in and the trees have grown tall and shady. Take, for one example, a modern, relatively new project on a tree-lined street in Westchester County, New York, within commuting distance of Manhattan. The development is probably typical of small, self-run communities of fewer than fifty units. One of the female residents wrote of that complex's troubles.

She said that at first, as each new family moved in, the sociability level rose. Every night there was a get-acquainted party. But as tenancy increased, cliques developed. One side wanted fences between the yards and the other voted no fences. And when it came time to elect members of the board of managers, the partisan campaigning was reminiscent of emotional high school elections.

That was in the complex's first four years. Then, tempers quieted down. Alas, so did everything else. Where there were willing workers in the first year of operation, committees then became desperate for members. General elections were merely perfunctory. Complaints to weary board members were answered with "You're absolutely right. Why don't you get on the board yourself and help out?" That scared away the dissidents.

She continued, "Some families moved and others have lost their enthusiasm for the real work involved in running a condominium. The board of managers must do the book-keeping, arrange for insurance, choose contractors for main-tenance, landscaping, painting, and so forth. They play the hard game of "Who is responsible?" which goes this way: Do I pay for my new underground garbage can or does the con-dominium? Our prospectus-makers (the nefarious builders) delighted in obscurity and omission."

Not a totally glum tale. Obviously the author is basically satisfied with condominium life—she stayed. But her words do point up the scattered annoyances that will come up from time to time to plague *every* condominium owner. There is always something bubbling in the complex: the dog problem, the owner who paints yellow lines around his parking space, and the one who wants the community's only awning. A resident of one adult community, a man who is now retired, said, "You have to be a conformist or you'll be very lonely." He had writ-ten, for a Sunday newspaper supplement, about some of the dissatisfactions of life in an adult community, about when bridge, golf, and craft classes begin to pall. "The reaction to that article was so bad that we were invited to leave," he recalled. "We received anonymous and obscene midnight phone calls and letters suggesting that we'd be happier living somewhere else." Note: He still lives in that community.

James Dowden of the Community Associations Institute in Washington, which dispenses information on the structure and workings of a community association, said, "Once you get over the problems of sudden immersion in the operation, that first two or three years when the assessment fee level is very vola-tile, it'll be all right." Dowden added that that comes about be-cause builders sometimes "low ball" the monthly maintenance charges initially to make the condominiums more attractive to prospective purchasers. They absorb the extra costs themselves. Then, when it's time to pass ownership on to the residents, the lid is off and the new owners face immediate higher maintenance costs.

Those buying into new buildings can have other problems. Sometimes a laundry list of construction faults can lead to lengthy litigation with the builder, during which time all tempers become frayed.

But even then, few residents storm out. The good points of condominium ownership appear to outweigh the bad. Norcross's study, for instance, found that over three quarters of the residents in his group interviewed are satisfied with condominium living at this stage of their lives. (Footnote: In the East the single-family home still remains the ideal. Satisfaction with condominium living is strongest in California, where 56 per cent of residents say they will stay five years or more. In the East that figure is 36 per cent.) What specifically did they like? In descending order of popularity, respondents cited: easy maintenance; dollar value; good neighbors; good design of the units; recreation facilities; the total environment; good location; security; and, lastly, privacy.

Several of those same attractions show up in the test group's initial reasons for buying a condominium unit. More than half made the purchase because they were tired of paying rent. To another sizable proportion, condominiums represented freedom from maintenance. Other reasons for buying, in descending order: the fact that condominium units cost less than single-family homes; better environment; recreation facilities; a greater feeling of security in the condominium complex; privacy, and, finally, friends that are near when needed.

SHOPPER'S CHECKLIST

When looking for a condominium unit a little more caution should be exercised than in house hunting. For all its claims, a condominium still means group ownership, and buyers are more or less dependent upon the builder and the community association to make their life reasonably serene. One must be wary, too, of developers with dubious building practices, who put up schlocky apartments, often minus the quality features that were promised, then fold their tents and are off. This scene has been especially prevalent in Florida and other resort areas where hundreds of condominium units have been constucted in the last half-dozen years or so.

There are obvious points to consider when comparison shopping—sturdy construction of the units, for example. But it is important for every woman to probe deeply into the workings of the complex to be assured that it is indeed as attractive a package as it appears physically. Hidden costs—and other traps —abound in a condominium. Here are a few special points to watch out for.

1. If the building or complex is new, check out the developer. Does he have a good reputation? Has he built other condominiums in the area that appear to be working well? What is his financial situation? If the community in which you are interested is several states away, you might write the real estate commission in that state to see if any complaints have been filed against him. For local or out-of-state purchases, check the state's Department of State and the Department of Consumer Affairs to see if either office has a file on the builder. You can even contact the U. S. Department of Housing and Urban Development's Consumer Protection Bureau at 451 7th Street, Washington, D.C. 20410, to see if it holds negative reports on the builder.

2. What are the builder's criteria for choosing buyers. Does he make background checks or is a hefty initial payment sufficient?

3. Watch your deposit money. If a specific number of units has not been sold by a cutoff date, will the money be refunded so you need not be tied to an unsuccessful development? Also,

down payments should be placed in an escrow account and not mingled with the builder's funds.

4.   Remember what was said earlier in this chapter about developers' practices of low-balling maintenance costs to make the complex more attractive to buyers. Don't believe the figures the salesman quotes. Ask for a detailed breakdown and then have a real estate pro look at the figures.

5.   The condominium association should have sufficient reserves to see it through unexpected problems without forcing sudden, high assessments on unit owners. If there is no extra money in the coffers, remember you will be assessed your share of any emergency repair bill. In condominiums that have been running for some time, ask to see the budget. You'll have to ask; this is not something that will be offered to you.

6.   Take your time signing a contract. What sometimes occurs in a seller's market is that you will be given a large packet of papers and told you must make a deposit of $1,000 or $2,000 or whatever. If you say you'd like to review the papers first, the salesman might say that's all right, there's a fifteen-day "cooling-off" period during which you can get your money back if you're not satisfied. It is true that in many states there *is* such a guarantee to buyers. But it is still better to look over all the condominium documents first and then sign, rather than the other way around. Also, you may want to negotiate a little and that may be difficult if you've already agreed in writing to whatever is in the sales contract. What if you want, say, a higher-priced carpeting or costlier kitchen equipment? These should be written in the contract *before* you sign.

7.   Does the use of the pool, tennis courts, and other recreational facilities go along with the cost of the condominium unit? Sometimes the builder retains control of those amenities and a unit owner is charged membership fees to use them. An executive buying an apartment in Florida ended up paying $1,200 a year for family membership in the project's golf and

swim club, an expense he hadn't counted on. That happens frequently. Sometimes the developer will hold a ninety-nine-year lease on recreational facilities inside the condominium complex —not even in a separate building. So you're paying to use your own ground floor. These practices are constantly being fought by owners' associations, especially in Florida, where the practice abounds. It is not illegal, however. An individual (or corporation) can, after all, under the U. S. Constitution lease his property to whomever he wants and for whatever purpose he desires, within the law. What might be possible however, is that the owners' association be allowed to buy out his interest, say, after ten years.

8.   Be sure that you can live with the condominium's bylaws. They all have their idiosyncrasies. Some adult communities, for instance, hold down to a certain number of weeks the length of time children under eighteen years of age may visit a unit owner each year. Women who expect to entertain young grandchildren often during the summer may be stymied by that ruling. In one instance, a condominium required all purchasers to agree to use the units only as second homes and that none of the owners would send their children to local schools. Similarly, there may be a restrictive clause in the contract about the age and relationship of occupants of each unit to the owner, or about pets or short-term rentals. Tenants may be prohibited from shaking out mops from the balcony or from barbecuing on it.

9.   Is parking free or is there an extra charge? Is the parking area sufficient? Since you and your neighbors will be having guests from time to time, there should be at least three parking spaces per unit, admittedly an ideal that is rarely realized. In one complex, owners sued the builder who promised them forty-seven spaces but built only forty.

10.   What about insurance? Usually there is common insurance for the common grounds, with owners taking out property and liability coverage for their individual units.

11.   Rentals tend to lower long-term property values. (In the Washington, D.C., area, for example, it is estimated that half of all garden or midrise complexes over five years old are occupied by rental tenants.) Renters are allowed in most developments and are only now beginning to cause consternation to the complex that finds itself in the unenviable position of landlord. The rental tenants usually do not know the workings of a condominium, its rules and regulations. They feel left out. Sometimes residents treat them as "second-class citizens." Remember that one part of condominium living that participants in Norcross's study found distasteful was renters.

12.   Naturally you will talk to as many residents of the condominium as you can before signing a contract. Ask, too, to see some issues of the condominium newsletter to see what, if anything, they've been bickering about. Sit in on meetings if you can. All of this mingling will also allow you to see if you can get along with these people and if your tastes are similar. Too much of a lifestyle or generation gap could cause squabbles over spending money or decorating or social programs or the lack of them.

13.   Generally, it is better to buy into an existing development than one that is still a hole in the ground, for the obvious reason that you can see what you're buying. Glossy sales brochures for the complex that hasn't been built can promise anything—and frequently do.

14.   Get *everything* in writing.

THE VACATION CONDO

A lakeside cabin or a bungalow at the shore still sound fine for getting away from it all, but there is a trendier vacation style these days—the condominium. Sprouting up in resort areas in this country and abroad, the condominium method makes perfect sense to travelers interested in far-off places but weary of overbooked hotels and expensive restaurants.

A stay at a resort hotel situated next to a condominium tower may set a vacationer thinking during those afternoon lolls around the pool. Both structures are handsome and beautifully landscaped. Both have swimming pools, tennis courts, restaurants, and perhaps even golf courses. There are shops on the street level of each. Why not buy a condominium unit, then, and save on vacation hotel bills? And with three-day weekends, it will be possible to get away for a few short visits during the year as well. There are other advantages to buying rather than renting or staying in hotels. You build up equity; there are tax benefits; and the property should appreciate in value. You may be able to rent it in your absence, too.

Those are the pros. Before plunking down several thousand dollars, remove the rose-colored sunglasses, settle down with a pencil and notepaper, and play devil's advocate to the plan.

First, will you become tired vacationing in the same place every year? Once you buy property in a resort area, you feel mighty guilty spending any free time elsewhere. Soon visiting that chic condo may become—is it possible?—a bore.

Take into account air fares, too, if your hideaway condo is in another state or out of the country. Two or three visits during the course of a year may be financially prohibitive, even allowing the trend by airlines in recent years of greatly reducing air fares. Other possible hidden expenses not often considered in the would-be buyer's initial wave of enthusiasm are for recreational facilities at the condominium. In many cases you must pay annual membership fees to use the pool, shuffleboard courts, golf course, etc.

Think about location. If you're going out of the country, how do the nationals there feel about Americans? What about that country's economic and political stability? Tranquil island paradises can become hotbeds of revolution at the drop of a palm leaf. In the mid-1970s, for example, terrorists went on a killing rampage on St. Croix, largest of the United States Virgin Islands. It appeared to be the sadly familiar story of a tourist boom bringing fortunes to investors while the island's native population suffered poverty and unemployment. Within two months after the murders began, condominium units priced at $70,000 had dropped to $40,000. Bad for the seller, great for the buyer. But who would buy, at least until the situation cooled down? Similarly, Jamaica's tourism income follows the ebb and flow of that country's political situation.

Tax advantages in owning a vacation condominium unit are the same as for a principal residence, in that deductions are allowed for the interest on the mortgage, plus property taxes paid to the local jurisdiction in which the condominium is located. If you rent your unit for part of the year, you may claim more.

But perhaps not as much as you may think. For many years taxpayers were taking advantage of business tax deductions from the use of their vacation homes by buying the houses, renting them for two months, and using them themselves for one and then filing for all the business tax allowances. Naturally, the federal government wanted to see that loophole closed. The Tax Reform Act of 1976 attempted to limit those deductions. It is an extremely complicated law, however, and you would do well to consult your accountant or tax attorney about how it would affect your condominium purchase. In general, though, the act makes the vacation condominium less attractive as a tax shelter.

It is not wise to count too heavily on rental income from your condo unit, although that is how the buyer frequently rationalizes her purchase: "It'll pay for itself because I'll rent it when I'm not there." Maybe. In a few projects, particularly in communities with a stable year-round population, owners' contracts may prohibit or severely limit sublets, to preserve the character of the community and to avoid transient traffic. Other places may have restrictions about the age of unit owners and, subsequently, of their tenants. Children may be prohibited.

The ability to rent your unit also depends on where it is located. If the area is glutted with condominiums, you are competing for tenants with many other owners, some of whom may live in projects that offer fancier amenities than yours. Seasons count, too. Presumably you will want to spend your vacation time at the condominium. If it is in the North, where summer is the peak season, and you plan to be there from August 1 to Labor Day, will the rent from June and July, say, $3,000, be sufficient to meet the annual operating expenses you had counted on a rental income's covering? Likewise, if you choose an isolated ski community that becomes a ghost town in the summer, you can pretty much forget about renting after the spring thaw. But a ski town with round-the-calendar attractions? Aha! Then you're on to something. In Florida and the Caribbean, too, the occupancy rates are evening out across the year. Naturally, January and February comprise the high season there, but visitors will come in off-season months to take advantage of lower prices—and rents.

Do be cautious when dealing with foreign developers who offer "all-expense paid" trips to their building sites. A discount on the cost of the flight or accommodations is reasonable, but totally cost-free inspection tours do not come without a hitch. At the least you will be subjected to a nonstop, high-pressure sales pitch that will make the one you heard at that free land-sales in New Mexico dinner seem like a gracious lecture by an Oxford don. At worst, you may find that somewhere along the line you've committed yourself to buying what they're selling and once back on home ground have serious doubts about the wisdom of that purchase.

For information about condominiums outside the United States, contact the American Embassy in the country in which you are interested, or its consulate or government tourist office in the United States to see how purchases there are handled. Several vacation trips to the area would also be wise before plunging into ownership.

Again, seeking the advice of an attorney and/or accountant

is important in completing any condominium purchase, but in negotiating with foreign countries and companies, it is *vital*.

Time-sharing

If a vacation condominium unit seems like too much of a burden, financially or otherwise, considering buying one just for your month's vacation. That is the latest spin-off of the condominium concept and it is called "time-sharing." Now about six years old, the practice works like this: You and a number of people buy shares in the same condominium unit. Those shares entitle each of you to use that condominium for a specified time of the year. Perhaps you will take the first two weeks in August. Allowing two weeks usually held open during the year for cleaning and repairs to the unit, there will then be a potential forty-eight other owners of that unit.

Time-sharing is a complicated ownership picture in that some plans involve shared ownership where each buyer gets title to an undivided interest in a particular unit, plus the right to use it for the specified annual period. Other plans involve vacation leases, that is, prepaid leases on particular units for the specified annual time. The term of such a lease can be ten, twenty, or even fifty years.

Drawbacks? Sure. Who is to say that the place will even be standing in thirty or fifty years, not to mention habitable? Time-sharing units will get greater wear and tear than conventional condominium units and the physical depreciation may be immense over the years. What happens if the "vacation club" that sold you your lease goes bankrupt? What happens if the building is condemned?

Also, you will have little to say about how the community is run, since your over-all ownership is minuscule—a small, fractional percentage in one unit with perhaps a thousand other co-owners. Since your investment is so small it is hardly worthwhile to take yourself off to Taos or Aspen or wherever to cast your vote in the annual condominium association election.

A time-share can be very inexpensive, though, certainly

compared to hotel costs in that location. Generally, 1979 prices ran from $5,000 to $9,000 or so for two weeks for however many years you like at a two-bedroom, two-bath luxury condominium unit that might cost you $90,000 to purchase. Expenses covering your share of utilities, insurance, linen service, and administrative costs will run around $75 a week. You will probably also have to make an initial outlay of $200 or so for your share of the furnishings for the unit.

You must sign up for a specified period of time, but that doesn't lock you into that slot in perpetuity. You can easily exchange slots with your co-owners or even with people in other complexes. Financing, if you need it, is by personal loan, not mortgage.

It is a gamble, since time-sharing is even less well regulated than conventional condominium sales. You are gambling on the developer's skill in building the complex, selling it and managing it properly, holding down expenses and maintenance charges, and, in fact, staying in business for, say, the next fifty years. That may be too much of a gamble—or you might figure your investment is at a low enough cost to make the roll of the dice worth the chance.

THE CONVERSION

The speaker is the not-so-pleased new owner of a condominium unit. It is, in fact, the same apartment in which she had lived happily as a renter for many years. As she put it: "I would rather have remained a tenant, but we have so many friends here it seemed easier to stay than to move. But think of all those dollars we hadn't planned to spend." She is referring to the $25,200 it cost to buy the apartment when it switched from rental status, plus the $500 she was required to pay for a parking space although she and her husband neither drove nor owned a car. Maintenance charges, the former tenant added wearily, are higher than the rent had been.

Condominium conversions are rampant. Builders recognize

the profit they can make in the switchover, while at the same time ridding themselves of the headaches and bad press that go along with being landlords. The growing rent-control regulations, they say, don't make owning rental property a good investment any more.

The owner prepares a conversion plan and submits it, where it is required, to local and state regulatory agencies; then the tenants see it. One realty man dealing in conversions advised other building owners how to approach tenants in a trade publication for the industry:

> Don't make mention of the change to condominium in advance; have all materials ready before making any announcement to tenants; explain everything to tenants in person, not by phone; give tenants about one week's notice before putting their units on the market; stress that the terms of their leases will be honored, but by another owner if they don't buy; try not to make an enemy of the tenant—keep going back, always politely and quietly, until you get a decision.

The tenant who would like to purchase her apartment when she hears the conversion plan is fortunate. She is buying property she is already satisfied with and is usually offered an attractive sales price, considerably—about $3,000 or so—lower than the one that will be listed later to outside buyers.

Then there is the tenant who does not want to buy. Developers estimate that only 20 to 30 per cent of the residents of a rental building stay on after conversion to a condominium or cooperative, so the unhappy people who want to remain renters are in the majority. Many of those tenants are elderly and have neither the money to buy nor the inclination to move. "I'm an old lady," said one tenant at a huge rental complex when interviewed about the rumor of a conversion there. "I lived here twenty-five years. But how am I going to buy this place? I got no money for that."

Tenants holding leases are usually allowed to stay on until

their leases expire; those without leases are often told they must either purchase their apartment within thirty or sixty days or move. The tenant who is being forced out does not have much recourse. If you find yourself in that position, *check first to see if your state has laws governing condominium conversion.* More and more do. New York is one state with a comprehensive set of laws—35 per cent of the present tenants must agree to purchase condominium apartments within a specified period of time or the offering is withdrawn. It may be submitted again a year or so later; usually at that time the price is lower. New Yorkers fight conversions with skill and bravado. In at least two very large Manhattan apartment buildings, tenants gave building owners such a rough time over a period of years that today the complexes are 50 per cent rental, 50 per cent condominium. In other buildings a small number of elderly tenants are allowed to stay on as renters. Washington, D.C., which has seen great conversion activity, has also strengthened regulations to protect the renter.

Tenants seeking clarification of their state's condominium conversion regulations can call their state's Department of Real Estate or Office of the Attorney General. These offices also handle harassment complaints if the landlord is getting abusive about your refusal or reluctance to buy your apartment.

Organized tenant resistance to conversion plans, if it does not defeat the proposal, can sometimes result at least in the developer's lowering the sale price of apartments or making a few other concessions.

Older apartments should be priced from 20 to 30 per cent lower than new, modern condominium units. This discount is fair since many older buildings have kitchens with no dishwashers or garbage-disposal devices—all pretty standard in today's kitchens—and in many cases no air-conditioning.

Buying into a converted building or buying your own apartment when the building switches has this advantage: you see what you are getting, you know the building's history, and know and can talk to its tenant-buyers. A tip to the outsider considering buying in: try to ascertain how many tenants are purchasing their apartments. That will give you an idea what its residents think of the building.

Many factors will enter into your decision whether to buy or move out when your building converts. Doreen's story is typical in that her housing choice was determined by several factors involving her job, her income, even her age.

Doreen, in her late twenties, is single and is an automobile salesperson. She recently settled in a Connecticut community, where she is employed at a Ford agency. Three weeks after she moved into a four-room apartment in a two-story, one-hundred-fifty-unit garden complex, she was told the development was "going condominium" and she would have to buy the apartment or move when her one-year lease expired. While looking at the apartment, she had been told there were no conversion plans, but . . . The builders offered her the apartment for $35,200. "Everyone told me, 'you'd be crazy not to buy it,'" she recalled. "I had only eighty or ninety days to think about the offer. I started asking about real estate up here and everyone was telling me how little saltbox houses were going for $90,000. Then two people wanted to buy the apartment, but I still waited. Toward the end of that time I thought, well, I'll buy it, but I'll have to borrow for the down payment and I wondered if I'd be able to get a mortgage.

"Anyway, they didn't bother me for an answer for *six* months, and by then the price had gone up $6,000. I blamed them for the builders not coming back to me during that time to tell me they were raising the price, but they said they didn't care because they could sell it with no trouble for more money." (The price Doreen had been offered for the unit was a lower one offered to residents.)

Finally, Doreen bought the apartment, based on these considerations: housing in her particular section of Connecticut was tight and expensive and rentals were high. The condominium style would probably be the most economical way to live. She liked her job, was doing well, and planned to stay in the region. She bought her apartment for $41,200. "I had to get a cosigner for my mortgage because my length of employment wasn't long and my income is in commissions."

Doreen did not plan to become a homeowner quite so soon; the role was actually thrust upon her. And she had never thought of buying any condominium, let alone the apartment in which she had been living. "I'm petrified," she said. "I really feel I have to budget my money now." She finds being a homeowner exhilarating, but says, "I never would have walked into this place and said, 'This is my dream apartment.' I'd never have thought of buying it. The complex is very plain-looking, nothing attractive about it, just brick, and not even enough parking spaces for all of us."

"But I know some of the people who bought here, so that's good. We're going to the first residents' meeting next week. And the owners are going to do some painting and landscaping and make some other changes. Across the street is a much nicer condominium project with units selling for $100,000. I think I could sell mine today for $45,000, and the way housing is going in this town, it can only go up more in value. I think I made a wise choice."

FOR MORE INFORMATION ABOUT CONDOMINIUMS:

The U. S. Department of Housing and Urban Development offers a free forty-eight-page booklet, *Answers About Condominiums,* which is available from the HUD Consumer Information Center, Department 586E, Pueblo, Colorado 81009.

The Community Associations Institute, 1832 M Street N.W., Washington, D.C. 20036, makes available, among other publications, *The Homeowner and the Community*

Association (65 cents) and *The Homebuyer and the Community Association* (50 cents).

The National Association of Home Builders, 15th and M Streets N.W., Washington, D.C. 20005, offers *Condominium Buyers Guide* for $1.00.

5

. . . And a Word About Cooperatives

It may lack the brushfire sweep of condominium construction and conversion, but the stock cooperative is another long-established ownership method that is now enjoying a revival. Today, several million Americans are living in cooperative housing programs of some kind. Many are nonprofit projects aided by government financing, but a growing number are in the private sector and can be very plush indeed. The latter had been almost entirely indigenous to New York City until the mid-1970s, but now cooperative buildings at all price levels can be found, for example, in Los Angeles, San Francisco, Boston, Chicago, Washington, D.C., and Minneapolis. Government-assisted co-ops, however, far surpass the number of cooperatives sold at open-market prices in those cities. Houston, New Orleans, and Atlanta still have little co-op activity.

The cooperative housing system is one designed to eliminate the builder's profit motive. It means ownership and control of a building by the people who live in it—not by a nonresident landlord. That building can be a typical high-rise that has been converted from rental status, or it can be a small factory consisting of loft apartments, or it can be a three- or four-story brownstone. Actually, just about any building can lend itself to cooperative ownership. Cooperatives are almost always found in urban locations, however—no garden complexes in rural settings so far.

In the cooperative method, you purchase shares in a corporation that owns the building and holds the mortgage on it. You do not own your apartment outright as you do in a condominium, but become a tenant-shareholder with shares of stock in the corporation equal to your investment and a "proprietary lease" that gives you the right to your unit. In conventional, or privately built, co-ops, leases typically run for the duration of the corporation. In publicly assisted buildings, they must usually be renewed every two or three years.

There are three major styles of housing cooperatives:

▪ The conversion or rehabilitation project, where existing units are being transformed by the landlord from rental status into a cooperative.

▪ The developer-sponsored project, built with private funds and with the intention of selling shares for all units to be run by the tenant-shareholders within two years or so after the first apartment shares are sold.

▪ The nonprofit or limited-profit cooperative, which is financed or otherwise subsidized all or in part with federal, state, or local aid and almost always made available to specific age or income groups.

THE EARLY DAYS

Cooperative housing, as we know it today, did not get underway in this country until as recently as 1920. Around that time a cooperative was started in New York City by a group of Finnish artisans calling themselves the Finnish Home Building Association. Although that may have been called a "co-op," it wasn't until six years later, however, that another project was erected that set the standard for future cooperative housing in the nation. That model project, also in New York City, was

sponsored by the Amalgamated Clothing Workers of America.
It was called Amalgamated Dwellings and was designed principally for union members. However, other occupational
groups were invited to join to round out the community.

The movement foundered during the 1929–39 Depression.
But then, after World War II, in the years from 1945 to 1961,
it became the most popular type of community housing in the
country. Its growth in Europe during those years paralleled
our own (it eventually outdistanced us). The early 1950s were
particularly significant years. In 1950 the Federal Housing Act
was signed, authorizing the FHA to insure blanket mortgages
on cooperative housing projects. One year later, the United
Housing Foundation was organized in New York State. Made
up of existing housing co-ops, trade unions, and other nonprofit
groups, it is an enormous organization that has developed more
than three hundred nonprofit cooperative buildings in that
state. In 1952 the Foundation for Cooperative Housing (FCH),
the nation's second largest nonprofit developer, was formed.
Based in Washington, D.C., the FCH has been responsible
for thousands of cooperative units nationwide.

It is important to realize that the cooperative form of housing has its own distinctive style, one that does not resemble
condominiums very closely. The condominium form can more
easily be compared to private homeownership than to the cooperative. The cooperative form is unique.

WHO RUNS THE CO-OP?

Residents of the cooperative structure, of course, run their
building. But at their head is a board of directors, composed of
from three to nine members, the majority of whom must be
members of the corporation. (In a building not sufficiently
sold out, the owner-sponsor will represent the unsold units,
which are usually by that time in the minority.) They are

elected by tenant-shareholders to serve two- or three-year terms. The board usually meets once a month. It enforces the corporation's bylaws and alters those rules when necessary. It considers new applicants to the co-op, keeps an eye on performance by the management firm, and votes on repairs. It becomes, you might say, the building's landlord. The board can make some decisions without consulting the shareholders; others require a vote, which usually takes place at an annual meeting. Each tenant-shareholder is entitled to one vote at meetings, whether he or she owns a penthouse or a studio apartment. ("Owns" is used, although "leased" may be more accurate because cooperatives *are* a style of housing ownership and most buyers certainly consider themselves home*owners*.) Day-to-day operation of the building, however, is usually handled by a management firm hired by the cooperative.

If you purchase shares in a cooperative, close attention should be paid to the makeup and workings of the board of directors and to its periodic reports. Board members are sainted souls with a thankless task, but remember, they may vote for new projects or purchases you may consider unnecessary or, conversely, they can permit the property to decline by keeping too tight a grip on the purse strings. Bear in mind, too, that a balance must be kept between changes you all want and those that can reasonably be made. In one converted building some co-op tenants wanted mail delivered to each door by one of the building's staff, and a manned desk set up in the existing mailroom, but both suggestions were rejected for budget reasons. One sharp, money-saving change, though, saw the doorman eliminated from a side entrance to the building and the tenants given a key to let themselves in.

In some publicly assisted co-ops that are subject to government regulation, more control may rest with the government agency than with the tenant-shareholders, although technically the cooperative owners are at the helm. Active participation by residents in that case is not always possible.

SALE PRICES

Co-op prices vary widely, often following the vagaries of the stock market or otherwise proceeding along a path different from the rises—and the reasons for those rises—in costs of single-family homeownership. What is particularly nerve-racking about the co-op market is that you may find an astonishingly low-priced apartment with astronomical carrying charges, or vice versa. In cities where co-ops are new and few, it is hard to comparison shop and judge the fairness of the co-op's price by others in the area.

Buying into a nonprofit co-op works differently. There, the purchase can be made for sometimes as little as a few hundred dollars.

THE MORTGAGE

Mortgage responsibility for the building rests with the cooperative corporation. There is one large mortgage on the building, or possibly two, which the corporation holds. Tenant-shareholders make payments on the corporation's debt on a prorated share basis—the larger and more elaborate the apartment unit, the higher the charge to that occupant. The co-op tenant's monthly check—called "carrying charges" or "maintenance fee"—to the corporation includes her share of the building's mortgage, plus taxes, insurance, and upkeep (repairs, staff salaries, management fees, and contingency reserves for unexpected purchases and repairs). With the exception of having to contribute to the building's mortgage, those expenses are the same as the ones found in a condominium.

FINANCING

Co-op stock purchases used to be a cash-in-hand transaction. There was no financing available at all, and indeed, if one

needed to borrow, he or she probably wasn't the co-op's type
of tenant. Banks were not sure whether cooperatives should be
considered real or personal property. The co-op lease and stock
shares were just not as good a security against default as a
deed on a home was. A few commercial banks were allowing
personal, uncollateralized loans to help toward purchase, but
the interest rate was high and the loans were usually extended
for only five years.

But then, in the early 1970s, a few states passed legislation
that would allow special co-op financing, usually at from 60 to
85 per cent of purchase price over from twenty to thirty
years and at an interest rate generally higher than that for a
home mortgage. Today, securing a co-op loan is not so trau-
matic and is not looked upon with disfavor by a co-op board of
directors, *if the loan is not too high*. Boards are still wary of
buyers who need too much financing, especially if those buyers
have no other assets.

One other point here. You will not be held personally ac-
countable if the cooperative for some reason cannot pay its
bills. But if you default on your co-op loan, of course, the bank
would get your stock shares.

MAINTENANCE COSTS

Unfortunately, the idea of buying into a co-op as protection
from rent increases was one bubble that quickly popped after
new co-ops had been on the market for a while. Maintenance
costs almost always go up, sometimes slowly, more often with
alarming speed. The reasons for the escalation are varied:
good old inflation, of course—rising fuel prices, higher wages to
the staff, higher cost for everything; original impractical estimate of maintenance costs when the building opened; new real
estate tax assessment, particularly if the structure has recently
been converted from a rental building; poor initial construction of the building, with glaring and eventually expensive defects just coming to light; and, in the case of an older

building, the inevitable malfunctions and needed replacements as the years pass. Rents rise too, of course, over the years. In cities with some sort of rent control, those increases are frequently held to 7 per cent or so. In a cooperative there are no such rise restrictions.

THE TAX PICTURE

As with condominium and single-family homeowners, co-operators are entitled to various income tax deductions for taxes and mortgage interest they pay for their share of the building. So, if you have a $400 monthly carrying charge and half of that represents your share of the corporation's mortgage, plus real estate taxes, that makes half your maintenance charge for the year tax deductible. If you have taken out a co-op loan on your unit, that interest is deductible, too.

SUBLET

Unlike a condominium, where the unit owner may sublet to anyone she chooses, provided the association allows subleasing, in a cooperative the person subletting and length the new tenant's stay must be approved by the board of directors.

RESALE

You may set the price and sell your shares in the co-op yourself, calling in any broker you choose. Sometimes the co-op board asks first chance at purchasing your apartment, but in any event, the buyers must, of course, be approved by the board.

In publicly assisted cooperatives, where there is frequently a long waiting list for admission, co-op tenants merely turn in their shares of stock in the corporation and are handed back the amount of their original down payment, any payments allocated to capital improvements, their share in the reduction of the mortgage debt, and a slight extra amount that could be considered "interest." The managers of the complex take care of selling the apartment. If the building is in an area where tenant turnover is slow, the co-op resident may be allowed to sell her shares herself. But since the purpose of assisted housing is to provide reasonably priced apartments from which no one makes money, what the shareholder may charge for those she owns is controlled, at least insofar as she may not walk away with any profit herself. If she sells for a higher figure than she paid, the difference is turned over to the corporation.

GOOD AND BAD FEATURES
OF CO-OP OWNERSHIP

The advantages of buying into a cooperative are similar in many respects to the condominium and to homeownership in general. By buying instead of renting, there is, first of all, no worry about rising rents (although, as we have seen, maintenance costs in co-ops appear to have their own escalating pattern). There are the tax benefits and equity buildup gained in ownership. The tenant-shareholder is free to make structural and major decorative changes in her unit without concern for lease restrictions or for tossing money down the drain on property she has no equity in. For the timid, a special, although minor, selling point of the cooperative over a house is that one need not sign one's name to a mortgage. In many respects the purchase of shares in a co-op is psychologically almost as effortless as moving from one rental apartment to another. Finally, there is enjoyment of a special camaraderie and pride that spring up among joint owners that is missing among the strangers who rent in the same building.

Disadvantages? Yes, there are some of those, too. A co-op is still apartment living and that often brings the usual gripes of noisy neighbors, too much togetherness, and so on. And then the co-op system has its own peculiarities. There is the politick-ing at the elections of board members and the feelings that usually run high throughout the year about those hardy spirits. The board complains about the tenants; the tenants are con-stantly bending a board member's ear with some grievance or other. Also, co-op residents must love their neighbors far more than condominium unit owners must since they are all tied to a joint mortgage on the building. (One concern that is useless to worry about, however, is that default of one of the tenants throws his or her responsibilities onto the shoulders of the others. That happens so rarely it is almost unheard of, yet it is a common worry of co-op shoppers.)

Then there are the arbitrary regulations that the corpora-tion's bylaws can impose. A "lease" may ban pets from the building, not allow sublets, or not permit tenants to have clothes washers. Perhaps there are rules about boarders and perma-nent guests that could upset a prospective buyer's long-es-tablished living arrangements.

The co-op board, as stated earlier, approves applications for new residents of the building. For tenant-shareholders, having potential financial deadbeats screened out is essential. But the practice has come in for charges of discrimination, since the board *can* select whichever applicant it prefers. Is there any kind of discrimination in cooperatives? Yes—on many grounds. It is not as bad as it was, say, in the late 1960s when the co-op market first took off, but it is still present. Not in every build-ing, of course. You will more likely be discriminated against on racial, ethnic, professional, or religious grounds than because you are a woman. You can fight what you feel to be a turn-down based on any kind of discrimination and sometimes you can win. If you find yourself in such a position and do want to file charges, contact your local commission on human rights.

Women buying into cooperatives alone do not face discrim-ination because of sex these days if they have the financial ref-erences and the ability to pay for the stock shares of the apart-ment. Elizabeth Stribling, a New York City real estate broker who has handled many, many transactions in what is the co-op capital of the country, says that women who must depend wholly or in great part on alimony for their income "would be given more scrutiny than someone who earns her own living," but that "there is really no blanket rule in co-ops. Each application is judged on its own merits. That may sound like just a catch-all phrase to ease out of a sticky situation, but it really makes sense. Someone who has $100,000 in assets but is earning $300,000 a year might be a better risk than someone who has $500,000 in assets and is earning $35,000 a year." (Admittedly, Ms. Stribling's buyers are in a *very* high income bracket! But you see the point she is making.) Ms. Stribling adds that a woman's best adviser, whatever her income, is her accountant; if he or she recommends buying into a cooperative, chances are good that the board would accept her application.

CO-OP SHOPPING

When looking for a co-op apartment it is important to read the prospectus carefully and to see recent financial statements of the building. How big is the mortgage? Are there reserves in the event of emergencies or is the corporation operating on a shoestring? Look at the co-op's newsletters to see what complaints have recently been aired—security problems, for instance. Naturally you will talk with as many tenants as you can, not merely to see if the building is running smoothly, but also to see if you will fit in with those prospective neighbors—age, lifestyle, etc.

You should do some comparison shopping, but that is not always possible in cities where co-ops are still new. Perhaps there will be just one or two buildings and that's it. A Hobson's choice.

Yes, when buying, you can haggle over price just as you would in a single-family sale.

Loft buildings can be a problem. Over half of those buildings in New York City, for example, are said to be illegally occupied. That means they do not come up to the city's building code and thus do not have a Certificate of Occupancy that makes living in any building legal. The loft building could have a few minor code violations or perhaps it needs a zoning variance to qualify for residential use. Some problems can be easily fixed and the C of O issued. Other problems take time to deal with and then . . . who knows? And there you are with a financial investment in an illegal residence. That's too much of a chance to take with your money.

For other points that should be considered when looking at cooperative apartments, read over the "Shopper's Checklist" in the preceding chapter (pages 65–69) on condominiums. Many of those tips can be applied by cooperative buyers as well.

And again, do not buy into this type of property without a lawyer. He or she should read the prospectus, the lease, and even the stock shares.

CO-OP CONVERSIONS

It is not difficult to understand why landlords are eager to convert their rental properties into cooperatives or condominiums. The buildings may not be making a profit, especially if they are rent-controlled and the tenancy shows no signs of moving. The structure may be deteriorating and capital repairs will soon be needed. To rid himself of the ownership headache, the landlord goes for a conversion.

What tenants find difficult to accept, however, is the often outrageous price they say the landlord asks from residents for what is sometimes a downright crumbling hunk of stone—and the fact that the conversion can usually proceed whether the tenants approve the plan or not. If they do not, out they go.

Regulation of cooperative conversions is minimal; in most states it is nonexistent. California and New York appear to

have the best rulings, New York in particular since cooperatives are more popular there than condominiums. In New
York, 35 per cent of the tenants must agree to purchase the
shares for their apartments within six months after the sponsor's prospectus has been approved by the state Office of the Attorney General. If the sponsor cannot secure that many purchasers, the plan is voided and cannot be resubmitted for
another eighteen months, at which time the share price has
usually been lowered.

One theory behind the preference in New York City for cooperative conversions over condominiums has been that it is
easier for landlords to transfer a large mortgage to an association than to individual condominium owners. Blanket financing for condo developments, with separate commitments for
each unit, means too much paperwork for lenders, with a limited mortgage interest return that can be charged to the unit
owners. The especially militant tenant groups in the city
charge that the real reason for co-op's popularity is racist and
that cooperatives give the landlord and then the co-op corporation control over who buys into the building, whereas condominium unit owners can sell to whomever they wish.

Besides offering the advantages of building equity to middle-
and upper-income tenants and the stabilization of their urban
neighborhoods through ownership, cooperatives have been
hailed by housing specialists as an alternative to rotting inner-
city dwellings for low-income residents, affording them a
means of homeownership. The conversion pattern in those
areas offers tenants government-aided financing plans and
"sweat equity" programs, whereby they physically work off
their financial requirements to buy into the building.

The switch from a rental building to a cooperative is not always accompanied by name-calling and knock-down fights between landlords and tenants. Some conversions proceed peace-
fully, some are, in fact, greatly desired, and a few are even
initiated by the tenants themselves. Here is one such story.

Marilyn and Larry loved New York City and their apartment in a handsome old building on the West Side. The street, unlike many in the area, is lovely and historic and is considered prime real estate. But a few years ago the couple had a problem that was blurring their Manhattan *joie de vivre*. With two small children, the couple were seeing the apartment shrink day by day. Should they move to a larger one and, as Marilyn wryly put it, "give up eating?" Or move to an established co-op which, at that time—a seller's market—would have carried an enormous price tag? Or should they throw in the rent receipts and take off for the suburbs?

They did none of the above. They talked to a few of their fellow tenants and generated interest in buying the building. When it was converted to a co-op, the couple reasoned, they would be able to move to a larger apartment or perhaps put two small units together for more space.

The small group of interested buyers chipped in about $50 each for a feasibility study (engineer's report) and for hiring a lawyer who would then approach the landlord. The lawyer did, and, yes, the landlord was interested—as indeed what New York City landlord would not be interested in a buyer for his rental property?

So he sold and they bought. Of course, it was all a bit more complicated than these few paragraphs—it took three years, in fact. During that time, Marilyn and Larry and a handful of other tenants held on to the idea, while others moved in and out of the building, quarreled, or lost interest.

When the sale was finalized, the co-op tenants had paid $850,000 for the thirteen-story building. The selling price of six times the annual rent roll was high, but one that is often charged in a prime location. Besides the purchase price, the West Side group put an additional $150,000 into a contingency fund for immediate repairs and improvements to the building. Fortunately for them, it was in pretty good shape; otherwise the fund would have had to have been larger. Naturally, not everyone was satisfied at the way things worked out. Some residents thought the purchase price was too high. A few, preferring to rent, moved out. But now the dust of transition has settled and those who fought for the conversion, especially Marilyn and Larry, are feeling rather proud of themselves. One point they had in their favor (besides sticktoitiveness): the building owner sold directly to the tenants. In some instances, a landlord sells to another real estate company that in turn "flips" the building to the tenants for a quick profit. These West Side tenants were in luck all around.

SUMMING UP

Cooperative or condominium? Here, at a glance, are the fundamental differences between the two apartment styles.

	COOPERATIVES	CONDOMINIUMS
Mortgagor	The cooperative corporation.	Each individual unit owner who borrowed money to buy his or her unit.
Mortgagee	Bank or other lending institution.	Bank or other lending institution.
Monthly charge (maintenance)	Proportionate share of the mortgage and all operating costs paid by each tenant.	Proportionate share of operating costs paid by each unit owner. Mortgage payments are made separately by unit owners to lending institution.
Real estate taxes	Assessed and paid on the property owned by the cooperative corporation.	Assessed and paid on each individual unit.

	COOPERATIVES	CONDOMINIUMS
Apartment	Bank loans—some-	Same mortgage rate
owner's mortgage	times called co-op	and terms as offered
	loans, sometimes	single-family home
	co-op mortgages,	buyer.
	usually at higher	
	interest rates than	
	home mortgages.	

FOR MORE INFORMATION ABOUT COOPERATIVES:

Co-operative Home Ownership: Getting a Piece of the Action, booklet published by the Brownstone Revival Committee, 65 Liberty Street, New York, New York 10005. Price: $1.00.

The National Association of Housing Cooperatives, 1012 14th Street N.W., Washington, D.C. 20005, has published a booklet answering commonly asked questions about cooperatives.

The Cooperative League of the USA, a national organization of housing—and health, credit, farm marketing, and consumer goods—cooperatives, publishes a good deal of helpful material. Write to them at 1828 L Street, N.W., Washington, D.C. 20036.

For regional information:
   California Association of Housing Cooperatives
   300 Valley Street, Suite 301
   Sausalito, California 94965

   Midwest Association of Housing Cooperatives
   343 South Main Street, Suite 208
   Ann Arbor, Michigan 48104

   Potomac Association of Housing Cooperatives
   C/o Multi-Family Housing Service
   6192 Oxon Hill Road, Suite 308
   Oxon Hill, Maryland 20021

6

Want to Buy
a $100,000 Mobile Home?

Did a double take at that figure in the chapter title, didn't you? But it's true—yesterday's grungy trailers have become sleek mobile homes that can cost up to $100,000. Naturally, with prices like that, the image of the seedy trailer court, with its shiftless and disreputable residents, has changed too. Driving through one of the newer, more expensive mobile-home "communities," as they are called today, a visitor sees little difference there from a suburban neighborhood of traditional single-family houses. There are wide, tree-lined streets in each; attractive houses set back on small lots and nicely landscaped. Mobile-home owners frequently add carports, porches, and decks to their units, making them even more indistinguishable from conventional housing.

More than 10 million Americans live in mobile homes today. About half are couples under thirty-five years of age and one quarter are retirees. The remainder is everybody else, and that can include a college-age woman whose parents buy her a $12,000 mobile home, where she can do her own cooking, for four years, in lieu of room and board expenses at school, to a divorced woman trying life and work in a new locale who prefers inexpensive homeownership to apartment rental.

(Incidentally, clarification is in order here. A mobile home is not to be confused with a motor home. The latter has an engine and riders can move freely between the driving and living areas.)

The old-style trailer courts made their first appearance on the American housing scene in the 1930s. The trailers were small units then, 12 to 27 feet long and 6 to 7 feet wide, with an over-all interior space of 100 to 180 square feet. Today's larger and more luxurious models feature more than 1,600 square feet of living space. Paul Goldberger, architecture critic of the New York *Times*, concludes that the better model mobile home "may come closer to satisfying a certain housing market than anything built today. It offers residents economy and privacy and yet the chance to have . . . a real house."

The increased popularity of mobile-home living over the last decade can be attributed to several social and economic changes in the American housing picture.

▪ Economy. In the last several years these homes have offered many Americans, especially young families and older persons on fixed incomes, their only chance for affordable homeownership. Despite that $100,000 price tag for flossier models, mobile homes generally run much, much cheaper. A single-width unit, nowadays measuring about 17 by 160 feet, costs from $9,000 to about $23,000 new and offers 1,000 square feet of living space. That price includes furnishings in any style—contemporary, Colonial, Mediterranean—carpeting and fixtures. The more deluxe double-width models, which consist of two units set back to back and feature such extras as fireplaces and bay windows, start at about $28,000. An even larger triple-width size, already seizing a good part of the mobile home market in California and other "sunbelt" regions, is beginning to make an appearance in other states. That model, which truly cannot be distinguished from a site-built house, costs from $55,000.

▪ Privacy. Since it is situated on its own plot of land, the mobile home offers greater distance from one's neighbor than a condominium or a rental apartment would.

▪ Community. The mobile-home park offers the buyer an immediate sense of community, which is often missing when buying into a single-family neighborhood or living in an apartment tower. The newer parks have clubhouses, pools, and keep-'em-moving social programs, even "courtesy buses" to local shopping centers.

▪ Easy maintenance. Mobile homes are pretty much maintenance-free, a feature that appeals to everyone, especially older buyers. Exteriors are permanently finished and interiors are usually completely paneled and carpeted. Said one woman, who recently purchased a $52,000 triple-width with her husband and teen-age daughter: "If we had bought an older house, we would have had to fix it up and change it around and we just didn't feel like that anymore. And we couldn't afford a brand new house."

So, as the price of new construction of conventionally built on-site houses continues to climb—it is now well over $60,000—more shoppers will turn to mobile homes. Over 70 per cent of single-family units priced under $30,000 today are manufactured, mostly mobile, homes.

Iris, who lives in a top-rated mobile-home community and is an officer of her state mobile-home association, feels that mobile-home living should be particularly attractive to single women or single parents. The homes require no upkeep, she points out, aside from washing down the outside once in a while. There is no need to worry about snow removal—that's taken care of by the park owner and, because the mobile-home community has no "through" traffic, it is safer than a city or suburban street. "You can walk here at night with no fear at all," she says of her park. "Your neighbors are always on the lookout, too, if they see anything peculiar. I know if I saw somebody poking around who looked suspicious, I'd do something about it."

Despite its success, however, the mobile-home world—both manufacturers and buyers—still has the problem of image—a public notion that mobile-home residents are transients and that a mobile-home park in a community lowers surrounding real estate values. What contributed to that view was the sight the public had been subjected to thirty or forty years ago of old trailer camps littering the main highways. The newer mobile home parks, somewhat off the beaten path, are usually hidden behind landscaping and do not offer the high visibility of their rundown predecessors. As for the "transients," a survey by HUD showed that the mobile-home owner's mobility is no greater than the population as a whole; that is, mobile-home owners move an average of once every seven years.

There is sometimes community opposition to mobile-home parks, but zoning variances and other acceptances are becoming easier, in part because of the attractiveness of the new communities, in part because of economics. Adult communities, in particular, are welcome in many areas these days since they do not place a burden on existing school facilities. Also, as the parks become more numerous and the mobile units more expensive, those who live in other types of housing tend to know someone who lives in a mobile park, perhaps in a better-looking house or one with better facilities than the conventional householder has. The two homes then become comparable. Mobile-home residents sometimes feel they must defend their housing choice, though, anticipating put-downs. One California couple living in a very posh Palm Springs mobile community carry pictures of their home around with them, so friends will see that mobile can mean very expensive indeed.

JUST WHAT IS A MOBILE HOME?

Legally, a mobile home is a motor vehicle, not real estate. Each unit has a license tag attached to its siding in some discreet location, and all have ditches dug underneath their bodies to accommodate axles, since if the axles are removed, some states no longer consider the homes movable and then they are taxed as real estate. The mobile home is assembled at a factory —there are some five hundred manufacturers—and trucked in sections to the park site where it is assembled. And that's usually the only trip the mobile makes. Fewer than 2 per cent are ever moved from their original location. So if you have visions of following the sun or working in different sections of the country, pulling your mobile home along behind you, better buy a Winnebago instead. The mobile does not travel. It *can*, but once it's planted, it usually stays right there and acquires a porch and carport and a deck and a few trees around it and a garden out back.

Can you buy a mobile home from the manufacturer and put it in the backyard of your conventionally built house? Exclusionary zoning laws usually say no. You'll have to check your particular locale. The same goes for mobiles homes set on vacant land you own. Some of the "manufactured" housing today *is* in the form of real estate, but here, again, regulations vary according to locale.

WHERE TO FIND MOBILE-HOME PARKS

Your state mobile-home association, usually located in the capital, will offer a statewide directory of parks. If you're looking specifically for retirement or adult communities and would like to relocate to another section of the country, write for *Woodall's Retirement and Resort Communities;* it is a listing available for $5.95 from Woodall's, 500 Hyacinth Place, Highland Park, Illinois 60035. Be forewarned that there will probably be just a few first-class mobile-home communities in your region (unless you're in California, Florida, or Arizona). If they are new and are still being built on, you will probably have no problem moving in. But in good *existing* communities, there is usually a waiting list for admittance.

If you have no luck locating parks locally, contact the American Mobile Home Association, 2680 Youngfield Street, Denver, Colorado 80215, telephone 303-232-6333. It can steer you to the parks you're looking for.

Prices for new mobile homes have been discussed earlier in this chapter. Resale mobile-home costs vary. In the top-quality communities some resales will bring higher prices than the owner paid initially. In parks of poorer quality, there will be depreciation of from 10 to 50 per cent. It all depends on the style of the community, its attractiveness, and its reputation. The last point is perhaps the most important.

There are "open" and "closed" parks. In the former, residents rent a piece of property and buy their own homes direct from any dealer they choose and arrange to have it installed. In a "closed" park, they must buy from the park owner, who generally selects one manufacturer from whom everybody chooses their models. That is not as bad as it may sound. In a closed park the owner can retain some control over the appearance of the park and can be sure that inferior models are not installed. Also, that manufacturer will have a variety of styles to choose from—buyers do not wind up in look-alike homes.

A tip to the budget-conscious buyer. If you can find them, look at mobile communities where the park owner expanded the older section of small units and began adding larger, more expensive models. If you buy one of the smaller, older models, you'll still be living in an attractive community and will have full access to any of the recreational facilities the owner may have added to beef up the quality of the park for buyers of the expensive models.

In addition to the purchase price for the mobile home, you will be presented with a lease that will require you to pay from $50 to $200 or more a month for lot rental, utilities, and upkeep. The lease is renewable and, yes, the rent usually goes up. Sometimes an entrance fee of several hundred dollars is charged, but in many states that is illegal.

FINANCING

The mobile home is financed like a motor vehicle, that is, with a personal loan. Interest rates are higher and the term of the loan shorter than with a mortgage for a conventional house. Down-payment requirements are also proportionately higher.

Mobile-home dealers offer financing, just as car dealers do. But you would do well to shop around before signing with one blindly. Their terms may be higher than you could find elsewhere. Besides checking out banks, try your credit union if you belong to one. Bank loans are from one to two percentage points lower than dealer loans. They run for from seven to ten years with down payments of from 10 to 25 per cent.

HUD's Federal Housing Administration insures loans made by approved lenders to mobile-home buyers who are able to make a small down payment and meet the monthly payments. The mobile unit must be used as your principal residence, and you must have a site for it acceptable to the FHA. The unit must be at least ten feet wide by forty feet long and must fit in with HUD construction standards. The FHA will insure this type of loan up to $16,000 for twelve years on single-width homes, larger loans for longer terms for larger models. The FHA requires a cash down payment equal to 5 per cent of the first $3,000 of the price, plus 10 per cent of the amount above that. Thus a mobile priced at $15,000 would require a down payment of $1,350. The Veterans Administration and the Farmers Home Administration have also been granted authority to include mobile homes in their mortgage insurance programs. The latter agency has not yet, as of 1979, formulated such a program, but you might give them a call. Perhaps they've put something together by now.

A few lenders have begun treating mobile homes as real estate and offering mortgages to buyers. The numbers of such lenders are expected to increase. In fact, the National Association of Realtors estimates that within five years from 30 to 40 per cent of today's installment financing of mobile homes will be real estate mortgages. Another tribute to the increasing stability and respectability of the mobile.

The reasons for the hesitancy in offering mortgages are, first, although the mobile is almost always stationary, it *can* be moved, and in that event, off goes the lender's investment if the mobile-home owner decides to be gone in the middle of the night. Second, until very recently all mobile homes depreciated in value, just as a car would, while conventionally built house values increased.

But as today's mobile homes are in better locations, are better built, better maintained, and more expensive; they do appreciate in value and many are sold for more than the buyer paid. In four-star communities, the seller of just about every house will realize a profit from the sale. So lending institutions can no longer make arbitrary decisions about the value of a mobile home. The housing style is changing too quickly for a knee-jerk "no" on long-term financing.

CONSTRUCTION AND SAFETY STANDARDS

Mobile homes are the only type of housing now required to be built to federal standards. Construction under HUD regulations calls for two exterior doors remote from each other; at least one egress window in each sleeping room; smoke detectors wired to the electrical system, with audio alarms outside each bedroom area; tie-down systems that anchor the unit to the ground; an electrical system that conforms to the one for on-site homes; and an increase in the fire-retardant rating for the surfaces of the furnace and water heater compartments and the area adjacent to the cooking range.

Mobile homes have long been called fire traps. A National

Fire Protection Association survey, however, showed that fires in mobile houses have decreased from 8 to 10 per cent in recent years, while fires in other types of residences have increased. As you can see from the HUD construction standards, every effort is being made to provide owners with safe units.

Another argument against the safety of mobile homes is that they can blow away in windstorms. Properly anchored—and that's the key phrase—they are as safe in storms as conventionally built homes.

PROS AND CONS OF MOBILE HOME LIVING

The advantages to this housing style have been mentioned. Residents of the better mobile-home communities are, according to surveys, happy with their choice. They like the communities' good looks, the comfort and ease of maintenance of their own units, and the social life in a mobile community, whether formally organized or in get-togethers among a few neighbors. But the housing style, like all others, does have its own special problems. For those leaving single-family homes there is the adjustment to "togetherness" living. You are a homeowner, but do belong to a community and must make concessions for the common good. Then there are the old feudal, landlord-tenant problems. You may own your mobile home, but you pay rent to the park owner to keep your unit on the ground that *he* owns. Rents go up. Some developers may be less interested in quality maintenance than others. One park operator, with a community of four hundred families, sold half his land, which had become extremely valuable over the years, to a commercial developer for a shopping center. Two hundred families were evicted. They had to move their homes to another location, whether or not they could find one. Park owners can make arbitrary decisions about the ages of children in the community, or about pets, or about any other petty or inconsequential item of daily life.

Mobile-home owners consider themselves homeowners, which they are. Yet they have landlords who can, within the law, do what they wish with their property. And there's the rub. In many states mobile-home owners have organized in much the same way rental tenants have—to protect their rights and, especially, to fight for legislation that will provide more protection for themselves and their housing choice. As mobile homes continue along their expensive upscale, they attract a better educated, more vocal, and more prosperous buyer. Some of these "tenant" groups already have earned reputations as tenacious, savvy fighters for park residents' rights. Also, as mobile-home communities become more attractive, a growing number of them are being forced by local legislation to pay real estate taxes. This development, a rather recent one, is forcing the industry actually to redefine the term "mobile home."

TIPS ON SHOPPING FOR A MOBILE HOME

▪ Talk to residents of the community in which you are interested to see if they're happy with their choice—or if they know of a better park. If you're buying a resale model and want to make a few exterior changes, will you be allowed to? Ask about garbage disposal, parking, transportation to shopping, churches, and schools. Does the community provide some of this? Is there an extra fee besides rent for use of the pool, shuffleboard court, etc.?

▪ Be careful about new communities under development that promise pool, clubhouse, co-op garden for residents, etc. If there's a cost overrun, or even without one, the developer may decide to drop those amenities in favor of adding more mobile homes to the community, and those niceties may never leave the sales brochure.

▪ The better communities frequently have newsletters. Ask to see a few copies. They will give you an insight into the kinds of people living in the park and their interests, so you can see if you will belong. They will also give you an idea of what the residents are grumbling about. Also, call your state mobile home association, which is composed of residents of most of the state's mobile parks. It may have regional tips for you and can explain state practices from the resident's point of view.

▪ And, of course, there's that old real estate golden rule: never sign anything without having an attorney look it over first.

▪ Finally, if you are unhappy with the park you have selected, you will almost certainly have to sell your unit, not move it. It costs hundreds of dollars to move a single-width mobile *if* you can find another spot to put it legally. House movers will usually not touch a double-width home, which is a risky move. But unhappiness with this style of life is unlikely in the better communities. Most of the folks there are very satisfied indeed with their unmobile mobiles.

FOR MORE INFORMATION ABOUT MOBILE HOMES:

Tips on Buying a Mobile Home, published by the Council of Better Business Bureaus, Inc., 1150 Seventeenth Street, N.W., Washington, D.C. 20036. No charge. You might try your local BBB office first.

The Manufactured Housing Institute, 1745 Jefferson Davis Highway, Arlington, Virginia 22202, also offers printed material for mobile-home shoppers and owners.

7

Housing Choices
for Special Times
of Your Life

For many, life's turning points are accompanied by fairly predictable housing choices. Marriage means an apartment, then a house, followed by a still better house. When the children are grown, it's probably back to an apartment, perhaps a condominium this time.

But life does not always work out that neatly. The traditional American family—working husband, nonworking wife, two children—now represents a mere 7 per cent of the population, while the number of single, separated, and divorced persons, as well as childless couples, continues to grow. So sometimes decisions are made from much narrower fields of choices, and many times there is no choice at all.

This chapter will consider divorced women with children, women who are widowed, and single women facing retirement, all of whom are facing changes in the way they are living. For many, if not all, of them, finances are the most important component of their new lives. Wherever they choose to live, price must be the first consideration.

AFTER A DIVORCE

One out of every three marriages in the United States in the 1970s ends in divorce. And for nonworking women especially, the emotional trauma aside, the problem of where to live on a reduced income looms large.

A house or apartment is frequently the visible evidence of that marriage, and all too often it becomes a battleground. An apartment is easier to break up than the burden of a house. Who will walk away with that house? Usually it is the husband who moves out, taking a small apartment and leaving the wife and children the larger family home. Most commonly, the wife gets "possession" of the house, but not ownership, until the youngest child leaves home. (Divorced women with no children and living in apartments are not considered in this chapter because for the most part it is easier for them to pick up their premarriage lives in the economic sense.) Then the house is sold and the couple divide the proceeds. If they are older, with grown children, the house is usually sold immediately and the profits divided.

If the husband has deeded the house to the wife, that can work to her advantage ultimately, although there may be some hard times until she gets on firm financial footing. The house may be too much to carry on alimony (if there is any) and a job that almost always pays less—and much less—than the husband's had. If she is lucky and can get through the expensive years of raising dependent children, she will, however, have a house. She is better off than the wife who gets half a house and must go through all that financial worrying and juggling and, when the house is finally sold, divide the profits. Her share may be small after the mortgage is paid off, the broker is paid, the closing and moving costs are paid.

If it becomes necessary for a formerly married woman to move to a smaller house, that can be unsettling, too. It is hard to scale down, especially for women who had lived, if not luxuriously, at least pretty well. That drastic cutback in income can be frightening, especially when the expenses of what suddenly takes on the appearance of a castle fall on her shoulders.

There are some 2.5 million divorced mothers in this country, triple the 1968 figure. Besides money considerations, their housing choices after the divorce are usually based on what will be best for the children—the neighborhood, the schools, the most space that can be purchased for the least price. And a few dozen psychological factors are poured into that cauldron as well.

Candy, to take one example, was divorced when her four children were still living at home and attending local schools. Since her only income was alimony and child support, she moved from a large house in an expensive bedroom suburb near a large city to a smaller house in the same community. She has been able to find a part-time job, but still is not sure she will be able to hold on even to that smaller home. "Divorced women really get hit," she says. "Unless you happen to be divorcing a man who has quite an income, you must go to work to maintain a house." Deborah was left with a small daughter and an eleven-room house that had been purchased in her name. She opened a decorating business, and with that income, plus alimony and some help from her parents, she was able to keep the house for three years after her divorce. But then one day she realized "it was ridiculous; I was spending about $1,000 a month just on the house." She sold it and bought a two-bedroom Cape Cod in a nearby community. She feels good about the move since she is on her own now and taking no help from her parents. Deborah feels that a house offers a sense of security. She did not want to "trade down" to an apartment. "If a person's life falls apart, she doesn't want to end up with nothing and that's what going back to a little apartment would have meant to me. If you lived in your own home before, it's emotionally better to go on living in a house. Then at least you have something to show for your life."

Like Candy and Deborah, most women who have lived in houses want to hold on to that feeling of ownership. But it is a complex decision to make. If you find yourself in this housing quandary—and this is after you have consulted a lawyer and are also aware of just what your postdivorce income is likely to be—consider these points:

▪ If you find that you are not able to remain where you are because you just plain cannot afford it, don't put off facing the fact that you will have to move. It can save you months of worry and aggravation. It is important that you not delude yourself into thinking you can maintain a $95,000 home on alimony, child support, and a $6,000-a-year part-time job—unless you have an inheritance to draw on or are taking help from your parents.

▪ Many divorced women move from the suburbs to the city. It is true that suburbia still appears to be couples-oriented, despite the growing number of single people moving into houses and condominiums there. Many formerly married women feel more comfortable in an urban situation. If the idea of city living does not appeal to you, of course, forget about it. But if you find yourself psychologically stranded on Lotus Blossom Lane, give it serious consideration. The move may mean a whole new life for you and can easily be less expensive to boot. Many divorced women find it difficult to maintain a suburban house and lawn and keep them in repair. A city apartment or co-op or brownstone can be easier to run. Workmen are, in theory at least, more readily available in the city and, probably most comforting of all, there are plenty of people in the city in the same boat that you are paddling along in.

▪ It is important for your morale that whether you move or stay put, you like at least one thing about your housing situation. If nothing comes to mind immediately, keep thinking until something does. Then hold on to it until you can make a move that will suit you better. With the other changes in your life, it is vital that your home, if not exactly what you want, is appealing in some small way. If you move, perhaps there is a working fireplace that you had always wanted in your new apartment. Or the apartment is so-so, but the neighborhood is good. If you are forced to move back with your parents temporarily, find one aspect of that arrangement that is a boon to you.

WHEN A SPOUSE DIES

For women who are newly widowed, housing decisions are of a different texture. Along with grief, there is frequently shock and disbelief, the feeling of living in a dreamlike state. One of the earliest decisions a newly widowed woman makes is to move. Frequently it is the wrong move, literally. At that time, anyway. But the overriding advice to widows—do nothing at first—is almost always ignored.

Lynn Caine, in her best-selling book, *Widow* (Morrow, 1974, $6.95; Bantam, 1975, $1.75), writes:

> Within three months after Martin died, I had given up our comfortable apartment in Manhattan, bought a house I hated across the river in Hackensack, New Jersey, pulled the children out of their New York schools and enrolled them in new suburban schools, embraced a way of life that did not appeal to me, that I was not suited for, could not afford and could not cope with. I was absolutely irresponsible and crazy. And even today I can't explain exactly what was going through my head.
>
> I was not prepared for craziness. But it was inevitable. Folk wisdom knows all about the crazy season. Friends and acquaintances tell the widow 'sit tight. Do nothing. Make no changes. Coast for a few months.' But the widow, when she hears the story, does not get the message. She believes that her actions are discreet, deliberate, careful, responsible.

Ms. Caine repeats the "sit tight" advice several times in her book, but she seems to know that that advice, even coming as it does from one who has been there, will probably not be taken. But a move that is well thought out and made well after the "crazy season" has passed can help a widow shift into a new life.

Liz Carpenter, who had been Lady Bird Johnson's White House press secretary, was widowed in 1974 after thirty-two years of marriage. She moved, too—a wise choice, as it turned out, but made after a couple of years' deliberation.

Ms. Carpenter and her husband had both had busy careers in Washington, D.C. But two years after his death she was "still racing—still not 'at home' in my own home. I was restless, nervous, lonely, miserable. I knew I had to change my environment completely. I thought about going home to Texas. The best of Washington for me was over, lovely and gone. I began to reason and weigh how I could make a permanent change. Financially, it would be easier to stay. The house was almost mine, payments down to $157 a month. I had a good job . . . and worked with good people [*Family Circle*, April 3, 1979]."

But she felt strange in the capital now, out of step. And on one particular visit back to Texas she began house hunting. Eventually, in Austin, she found what she considered the perfect house and has since delighted in decorating it to suit herself. She has settled in, she feels, and has found—with the house, friends, and a new job—exactly what she had made the move for: a new life.

Most older widows—older women generally—prefer to remain independent. The Census Bureau in 1976, reporting on widowed Americans over sixty-five, stated that just 4 per cent of men and 13 per cent of women lived with a relative.

The advice to widows to wait before making a move is made, of course, to women who can afford to remain where they are. Some cannot. There are more than 10 million widows in the United States today. The majority are over sixty-four years of age, but over 100,000 are under thirty-five, and another sizable number are from thirty-five to sixty-four years old. Many of those younger women have dependent children. They face some of the same housing problems as divorced women, perhaps worse if they were left with inadequate insurance and do not work outside the home. With no alimony and child-support payments to count on, they can be plunged into an even deeper financial abyss than divorced women. Sessions with accountants can give them clearer pictures of their finances and what type of housing is best for their income.

If you are a young widow with children, several of the points divorced women should consider, stated earlier in this chapter, can apply to you as well.

AS YOU APPROACH RETIREMENT

Retiring these days does not mean retiring from anything but that nine-to-five job. But too often it is approached, if not with downright anxiety, then with a certain apprehension of what is to come. Financially, will you be able to stay in your home? Will you want to? If you are married and your spouse dies, where will you go? Retirees have many years to plan for that event, and most of them do, very carefully. There is time to consider the pattern of rising rents or real estate taxes where you live and to make note of outside expenses that will take up more and more of your pension dollar. Social security and pension allowances are figured out by most down to the last nickel.

Some folks who retire are happy to stay put where they have lived for years, close to family and friends. But others want to cast off the old and head for, to them, unknown territories, new housing styles. Moving to another section of the country is a popular decision. Most of those moves are successful—the retirees find affordable housing and a style of life that is everything they had hoped for in those preretirement years. But sometimes the reality of relocation is less than what was bargained for and the retiree comes back home. What went wrong? Here is what some returned transplants who have just unpacked their suitcases in or near the old home town have to say.

Frances moved back North from Florida after the death of her husband because "I was alone down there. All my family was up here and my daughter was worrying about me."

Charlotte and her husband Elmer returned North from the St. Augustine area after only four years because they missed their four children and thirteen grandchildren. "It was just too far," Charlotte explained, adding that "nobody was able to make that many visits back and forth."

Others simply did not like life under a brilliant sun. Especially the sun. "The heat was so intense and the bugs would drive you out of your mind," said one retiree. "Unfortunately, we weren't in a position where we could come up North four or five months during the summer and it just got to be too much."

The heat finally got to a woman who lived in Scottsdale, Arizona, almost eighteen years before moving back North: "I didn't like the desert; I love the green and the ocean."

"We found life quite dull," said a woman who left Florida with her husband. "People there seemed to have nothing to do except sit around all day and talk, or just stare into space."

All of those who made a drastic move on retirement advise retirees contemplating a permanent life several states away to spend more than a week or two vacationing there—no matter how many years of such brief trips are involved—before plunging in and buying. See how life is in the desert in August or in New England in February. Don't just visit in the tourist season, when everything is lovely. That is not representative of day-to-day living in that region.

Moving South is often done to ease living on a retirement income, because of lower living costs (lower fuel, a one-season wardrobe, etc.). But if you want to stay home and cut back on expenses, there is a new device called a "reverse mortgage" that may be able to help. If your home is paid for you can use that house to gain income. The reverse-mortgage principle takes the equity in your home and transforms it into a running income for you. You continue to live in the house as long as you like. What you get from the lender is a loan where you receive the proceeds either in a lump sum or in installments. But you do not repay the loan in stages as you would with a mortgage. Instead, the lender is repaid only when you sell the house or die. If you sell, a part of the money received will go to repay the lender. If you die, the house is sold, with the lender repaid and the balance of the profits going to your heirs. Interest rate is usually the same as for conventional home mortgages. There are several variations of this program; for the retired it is an interesting concept. At this writing, reverse mortgages are granted in only a handful of states, but the program may be available nationally as you read this. Check the mortgage department of your local bank.

Another means of reducing your expenses—and certainly not everyone will be able to take advantage of this—is to will your house to a local college or university or private school. Under the usual arrangements of such a bequest, you will be allowed to stay there until your death, and in the meantime the institution will pay all or part of your fixed expenses—property taxes, say.

A TAX BENEFIT

Remember, if you are fifty-five years of age or older at the time you sell your house, and it has been your principal residence for at least three years in the five-year period preceding the sale, you can exclude from income up to $100,000 of any profit on the sale of that residence. And "residence" includes condominiums, cooperative apartments, houseboats, and mobile homes. Before July 26, 1978, you had to reinvest the profit from that sale into another residence within eighteen months or pay a hefty federal capital gains tax. But today you can take the $100,000 profit without paying that tax. This is a one-shot, once-in-a-lifetime deal. If you make, say, a $60,000 profit, you cannot use the remaining $40,000 in a later exemption. So choose the time you sell carefully, and the dwelling you are moving from, too. If you are fifty-three years old, it may pay you to stay put for another two years. This law is already affecting the buy-sell patterns of the nation's retirees and soon-to-be-retired.

UNIQUE
HOUSING ALTERNATIVES
FOR ALL AGES

Whatever your age, marital, or employment situation, the move need not be to another house or condominium or rental apartment by yourself. Imaginative solutions are being found for women who cannot afford to live alone or who do not want to do so.

Sarah has been a widow for more than a year and feels she must decide on a housing style for what she considers will be the rest of her life. She is sixty-three, has no family or distant relatives left, and is fairly comfortable financially. But she does not want to live alone. On the other hand, she does not want someone living with her who will be dependent on her. What should she do? Well, Sarah lives in Chicago and she contacted what is called the "Share" program there, which operates out of the Jane Addams Hull House. It is for seniors who are looking for someone to share their apartment or house, or vice versa. Sarah found someone suitable through Share without having to advertise, which could have brought forth nuisance applicants. If that type of arrangement appeals to you—and for some women it may be the only way they can keep their homes—contact your nearby senior citizens center or family service agency to see if they have similar programs. If they do not, perhaps your joining your senior center will put you in touch with women who would make good candidates. In larger cities there are placement services which, for a small fee, bring sharers together. These services are usually reliable and do an effective job of preliminary screening of candidates.

Although aimed at the young and new in town, the agencies are taking on more and more older applicants as housing costs rise.

Another program in practice in a few communities uses federal monies to help retired persons on certain limited incomes convert half of their homes to rental units, thereby halving housing costs. This can be done only where zoning permits it, of course. For more information about this, get in touch with your local Community Development Agency or HUD office.

Still another development in housing styles is creating new "families" composed of friends who live under the same roof. Consider: A divorced woman with two school-age children does not, for various reasons, want to stay in the suburban home where she once lived. She moves to a large house in a metropolitan area with two women who also have children. The house then becomes affordable to all of them. The children have built-in companionship and three adults keeping an eye on them instead of being frequently alone in an empty house, and the women have the city living they want. Old city houses especially lend themselves to this form of sharing. Sometimes each adult has a separate bedroom and the children share the remaining sleeping quarters. Sometimes each adult shares a bedroom with her own children. The kitchen, dining, and living rooms are communal. If a house is already divided— or can easily be—into separate full living units, so much the better: an apartment for each family group. In communal living in a house all adults chip in the same amount for the down payment, and all expenses—mortgage, taxes, insurance and repairs—are split evenly.

Your local Parents Without Partners chapter might be good hunting grounds for people interested in this type of arrangement.

Besides being a good idea for single parents, the shared-house situation can work for women at or nearing retirement age, too. Each can have, say, a bedroom and sitting room, and the other facilities can be shared. Three women, each living alone in a $70,000 house, can, for companionship and economy, sell their separate houses, join forces to buy one large $100,000 house, and still have a nice bit of change left over for themselves.

LIFE CARE

Life care facilities, representing a relatively new housing concept, go back to the 1930s, but a renewed interest in them appeared about a dozen years ago. New ones continue to open around the country, although there is no count of exactly how many are in existence. The facilities, which usually resemble handsome high-rise or garden apartment complexes, are open to those sixty-five years of age or over. Besides apartment units, they feature a central dining room, a health center, perhaps an outdoor garden, and shops. But the most important aspect of life care is just that—you are cared for in these complexes for the rest of your life. Residents receive full medical services, which include physician visits, nursing, surgery, hospital care, prescription drugs and physical or occupational therapy.

There is usually an emergency call system that connects all apartments to the health center where nurses are on duty around the clock.

As you have probably guessed, life care does not come cheap. Costs of the apartments range from $20,000 for an efficiency unit to $50,000 and more for a two-bedroom unit for two apartment occupants. After paying the initial buying fee, a resident pays a monthly service charge, like rent or a condominium maintenance fee, which varies but generally starts at from $400 to $500. That fee covers all living expenses, including health care services, three meals a day, weekly housekeeping, linens, building maintenance, security, and utilities.

Most life care facilities are sponsored by religious denominations, although they are, of course, nonsectarian in operation. The better ones have long waiting lists. The occasional proprietary (operated for profit) project frequently runs into problems. "People are not willing to give those sums of money to a proprietary group," said one observer close to life care administration.

A good facility will be praised by its residents as the best housing choice they ever made. But there are problems with life care, too, even with the best of them—problems that are only coming to light as the principle becomes more popular.

What happens—not always, but often enough to loom as a major obstacle to successful life care administration—is that those monthly charges rise the same way that rent and condominium charges go up. In one community, over a period of ten years, the fees have risen from $430 a month to $1,600 a month. That kind of increase could cause a young tenant great worry, but to a life resident it could be catastrophic. Several nonprofit life care facilities have gone bankrupt, too. They are then taken over by proprietary groups who—because they have to or want to—raise the monthly charges.

Most of the legislatures in states where life care retirement homes went bankrupt subsequently passed laws regulating the life care industry. In Florida, for example, there is now a law providing strict regulation of the industry. Future life care corporations are required to undergo state audits and maintain set levels of reserves.

Finances are the main problem of the life care industry. Unlike buying a condominium or cooperative, where you the buyer can examine the books and do your best to see that the seller is financially solvent, life care facilities do not now offer that access except in states requiring it and they are few.

If you are considering moving to a private retirement home, do all that you can to find out the corporation's financial standing. Talk to residents there, of course, and not to those who moved in just six months ago. Many a sixty-five-year-old has lived in some of the older facilities for ten years or more. They are the people who will know all there is to know about the facility. Contact your state office on aging or Department of

Health for a list of health care facilities in your state and for an indication of how they are regulated where you live, if they are at all. People are living longer these days. If you move in at sixty-five, you may be living there twenty years or more. Like housing communities of any age group, life care facilities have their core of bright, articulate, aware residents who are campaigning to see their housing style become more secure, better regulated, and thereby more pleasant for all of them.

Louise, an eighty-six-year-old woman wrote in the New York *Times* of her experiences moving with her eighty-eight-year-old husband to a retirement home. She wondered if they could adjust to living in a retirement home since, to her, the idea brought to mind a tree loaded with sparrows and unending days of gray monotony. The couple had prided themselves on being individualists and wondered if they could, as she put it, "submerge ourselves in some geriatric human warehouse."

There was no need to submerge. The couple—amazingly, they felt—slipped into their new life with ease. Forming new habits and meeting new friends—all of it they found exhilarating.

As they neared the end of the first year in their new home, Louise said that her husband asked her where she "stood" now.

She answered, as she had during all their time in the home, that she is "still with it."

"We had gambled on our future," she concluded, "and I still believe it was a good bet."

And it can be for you, too.

FOR MORE INFORMATION ABOUT LIFE CARE:

"Directory of Life Care Communities," a listing of facilities nationwide, is available for $5.95 from Kendall-Crosslands, Box 100, Kennett Square, Pennsylvania 19348.

8

Can You Swing
a Vacation Home?

If the American dream is to own a house, that ideal carried a little further is to have a second home as well. Many a vacationer has returned from a rented shore bungalow with visions of her *own* little cottage—nothing fancy, just a beach shack really. Or she is home from the mountains with a suitcase full of —no, not T-shirts and souvenir ashtrays—brochures touting condominiums and chaletlike developments at every mountain's base. The lure is the same: a place to get away from it all, to relax, unwind, and put the pieces together before the next week's assault. And, of course, to rent to others whenever one chooses so that the little hideaway pays for itself.

The vacation home market went through a bad spell during the 1973–74 fuel crisis and construction downturn, but it has rebounded and is now healthy, it is to be hoped, the 1979 fuel crisis notwithstanding. Demand is high as more and more two-income families go house hunting. Some 3 million Americans own vacation homes, based on the 1970 census. That figure should rise appreciably when the 1980 census figures are released. Most of those buyers had been considered affluent older persons, but that profile is changing. Second-home owners are usually in the forty-five to sixty-five age bracket, but in the last couple of years more are at around age thirty-five. Most buyers have a median income of $36,000 and are people with professional, business, or managerial occupations. The majority of buyers have their principal residence near their second home. A Cape Cod real estate broker explains the lure of his region, which holds true for many other vacation spots: "Basically, customers are looking for a seasonal home near the ocean with minimal maintenance. The low maintenance is a popular feature—in fact we've become known in this area for 'weathered shingles,' which means no painting. Most of our buyers come from the surrounding area because they want to be able to drive to their second home. Lately we've been selling resort properties to singles—both male and female. A typical single customer is someone with an apartment in the Boston area but who doesn't want to own a home there. We get many teachers from the city who want seasonal homes on Cape Cod."

Any type of dwelling can be a second home. Beach houses and mountain cabins most often come to mind, but the hideaway can be a condominium or farmhouse or a log cabin or converted one-room schoolhouse. For those who live in the country year-round, a second home can be a *pied-à-terre* in the city. In fact, it is any dwelling that you do not, for voting and tax purposes, consider your principal residence.

The prices of second homes have risen sharply in the last decade, just as they have for other types of real estate, although the average second home still runs about $10,000 less than a primary home. For a second home, a buyer can expect to pay perhaps as little as $16,000 for that good old "handyman's special" that needs work to over $100,000. Want a condominium unit in Vail, Colorado, within walking distance of the ski lifts? A one-bedroom apartment will cost you around $90,000. It is equally expensive to be near the ocean or lake or whatever the attraction is in the area in which you are interested.

Second homes are purchased for reasons other than just fun in the here and now. Some are bought as eventual retirement homes, with the buyers spending more money on the houses and more time in them as years pass, until they move in permanently. Many houses are purchased with the expectation of rental income and future sales profit and are not even used by the owners.

What Do You Want in a Second Home?

Well, we all know what we would *like* in a second home. But let's be sadly realistic. First, what do you expect from that home? The ability to leave a city office at 5 P.M. on Friday and a few hours later be walking along a beach? To spend winters in a warmer climate? To ski two weeks out of the year? If it is the first, you will get plenty of use from your house. If the second, that home or condominium will probably be vacant nine months or so of the year. Can you afford to carry it if you cannot rent it during that time? If you just want to spend your two-week vacation there, buying a second home might be too much of an investment, financially and otherwise, for you. You may be better off staying at a hotel or renting a condominium during those two weeks.

(We are not talking here about investors who buy many properties for tax shelters, but of ordinary homeowners looking for a second home for fun or as a short- or long-term investment.)

The highest prices in the area you select will be for traditional houses that are usually year-round residences. And these will be very high. Condominiums and townhouse communities in recreational areas are also priced high, unless there is a glut of them in that particular market, in which case you might benefit from a price war. Somewhat cheaper would be your purchasing a lot, then having a contractor build a specially designed house, either to your plans or his. A deal like that calls for very careful reading of the sales agreement. There is more on buying raw land in Chapter 11, on investing.

There *are* cheaper houses around, if you head for the woods and small, off-the-beaten-path villages in counties that have not yet become chic. The search may take a year or two or three, but finding the right second home does take longer than buying a principal residence. Keep an eye open for the offbeat property. Since this is a vacation house, you can afford to be a little unconventional. Maybe there's a small church, firehouse, train depot, or barn that you could convert to make a perfect home. Read some of the books that have been published in the last few years on alternative uses for existing buildings to see how many of these properties have been imaginatively converted to residences.

As you are reading this, consider fuel costs and air fares to your Shangri-La. Are they rising? Likely to remain steady for a while? Dropping? Many house hunters look no more than ninety miles from their primary residence, both for less expensive traveling and the ability to spend more time there. It is difficult to weekend in Vermont frequently anyway, if you live in New York City.

Bear in mind, too, that in some resort areas where several new communities are being marketed simultaneously—the Pocono region, in eastern Pennsylvania, is a good example—you will be subjected to high-pressure sales pitches as you go from one development to another. Salespeople for these complexes are sharp and can turn your 'we'll see' into a signature on the dotted line in the time it takes a pine cone to drop. Read over every line of these contracts before you sign and have a lawyer look at the document too. There is a lot that can go wrong before that sea of mud becomes Woodsy Mossy Acres. Ask about the water and sewerage where you are planning to buy. This is important in the mountains because drainage there is often not good and sometimes will not support large septic systems. If the land you are considering will, how many tanks will you need? How good—or bad—are the roads leading to your property? How quickly will they be cleared of snow in the winter? If you plan to spend weekends there and leave early Monday mornings, via your own or public transportation, will you have to worry about being snowed in? And what about that public transportation?

Spread yourself thin when looking at existing homes by registering with several real estate agencies rather than just one. The market is tight, and while a multiple-listing service will offer everyone most of the same properties for sale, you never know when an exclusive listing will come in that is just what you have been looking for.

When looking at little bargains that need much work, ask yourself how you want to spend your getting-away-from-it-all time. Sitting in the sun is the most some people can manage, while others relax by practically rebuilding a house. If you live in the city, the idea of hearing nothing but crickets at night may sound appealing. But if you live alone or have small children, the wilderness may not be safe. Vacation homes in remote areas are inviting targets for vandalism and serious thievery and can even be taken over by squatters if the house is not visited often by its owners. Tenants for the times you're away might be put off by an isolated location. If you *must* live in God's country, the house that at most is five miles from town is a better buy than that one that is really in the boondocks, come resale time.

Can You Afford It?

Carol and Dee are journalists who work in Manhattan. Both went house hunting—separately—and both purchased, as most of us do, a little less than they had hoped for. And it was pretty convoluted shopping. Dee's annual salary is $35,000. She had been living in a $450-a-month rental apartment in Manhattan and felt the time had come to invest in some sort of real estate. She spent nearly a year shopping for a cooperative, but found nothing appealing. Not at what she could afford, that is. Then, during a tax session with her accountant, she learned from him that for cash flow and tax deduction purposes, she would be better off buying a vacation home and remaining in the apartment. "I needed the money," she said.

"Cash flow sounded good to me." So Dee, who is divorced and in her thirties, purchased "a dinky little house" in Westhampton, Long Island. Does she now have the best of two worlds? Not exactly. She cannot afford to live in the second house. She fixed it up "as chic as I could make it" and at this writing is renting it for her first season at $1,400 a month, June through August. That's $4,200 and it costs $6,000 a year, or $500 a month, to pay mortgage and taxes on the house. Dee is now looking for winter tenants, which she stands a fifty-fifty chance of finding, since there is little life in the Hamptons in the winter. However the accountant's advice works out—and for cash flow it is dubious—and however well or poorly Dee does in renting the house, a house—any house—in the Hamptons will appreciate rapidly, and the land is of course valuable.

Carol is a free-lance writer, a single, in her thirties, and earning $24,000 a year. She had been living in a Manhattan apartment, too. Her plan was to purchase a two-family house on the New Jersey shore with her parents, who were retired and living in that state. The older couple would occupy one apartment and Carol the other. Since her parents would be there all the time, they could also keep an eye on the property, Carol reasoned. She herself would be there autumn, winter, and spring weekends, but she would have to rent her unit from Memorial Day to Labor Day.

But on house-hunting trips the eyes of Carol and her parents opened wider. The *prices* for shore property! And this was blocks in from the beach. Even the worst hovels were going for $60,000. Zoning laws forbade converting single-family houses into apartments, so they could only look at existing two-family homes. The problem here was that Carol's parents, since this was to be their primary residence, understandably wanted an attractive house in a good neighborhood in one of the better communities, while Carol would gladly have bought a more casual beach house in a community rated just a bit lower on the social scale. She did not want to move into the house permanently because, as a free lance, she felt, psychologically anyway, that she should be near the New York publishers with whom she dealt. Her elderly, rent-controlled Manhattan apartment cost $200 a month, so Carol expected one half of a nice $55,000–$60,000 home was an expense she could carry.

After a few disheartening trips to various communities, and a few disheartening talks, Carol and her parents made a few decisions. Carol purchased a brownstone in Brooklyn—a duplex for herself and two rental units. Her parents sold their large house in New Jersey and moved to a garden apartment complex near their former home. Carol hopes that one day they will move into one of her apartments. She is happy with her choice, although during the summer she still looks covetously at shore properties she cannot afford to buy (and that is just about every one of them). She cannot pass brokers' offices there without checking the listings in their windows. The prices!

So there it is again—the trade-off. It is becoming more difficult—unless you live in a two-income household—to swing a second home *and* be able to live in it from time to time.

Unless—a few friends join forces and buy a property together, turning it into separate apartment units for each or converting it to a condominium or cooperative. Or you can buy a piece of land today; then, in a few years, when your income is higher and you have managed to save a few dollars, you can build an inexpensive house on it, perhaps a manufactured A-frame or log cabin. Or you can find one of those $16,000 bargains, one that does not require another $35,000 to make it habitable.

Do not feel if you spend $3,000 renting a summer home at the lake that it's money down the drain and you should buy there. As you see, buying is not always possible—in fact it is usually *not* possible. Even if you did rustle up the down payment, banks are careful about mortgage money for second homes. They will take into account your mortgage and taxes for your principal residence or your rent there, and if your income is not sufficient to support two residences, you will simply not get the mortgage. Your planning to rent the house seasonally does not carry weight with mortgage loan officers.

In general, mortgages are not difficult to obtain for those who can afford homes, although down-payment requirements are usually higher and the length of the mortgage is cut in half —ten or fifteen years is common. To raise the down payment you may be able to refinance your existing home, if you have one. That will depend on how much equity you have in it. Some buyers go into hock to buy a second home they feel will be valuable to developers in a few years' time so they can collect a bundle, and sometimes they do.

Finding the money to buy is only one of your potential headaches. Surprisingly, finding the house itself may be your first problem. Construction has slowed down somewhat of late because of high interest rates and the rising cost of building materials. Environmental rulings are keeping more houses and condominiums from being built in settings that could be considered recreation land or land that should belong to the public. And there is only so much oceanfront and only so many houses that can be built facing lakes. Most of the valley floor at Vail, for one example, is already developed. So real estate prices there can be expected to rise, unless the region is overbuilt, a situation that exists in South Florida and Ocean City, Maryland, to name two resort areas in that predicament.

Also, if you are depending on your tenants' rent to pay all the expenses of your home, you may have to rethink that strategy. The National Association of Home Builders estimates that 40 per cent of the people who have vacation homes try to rent them at one time or another, with varying degrees of success. If you are going to count heavily on *seasonal* rentals, you may be in for a disappointment, if not financial disaster. A year-round rental is more likely to cover your expenses.

Part of a developer's sales pitch at many resort condominiums is probably that he will find tenants for you. How does he know he can, for sure? In some areas, referring again to glutted South Florida, how can you be sure your lone condo in a sea of thousands will be booked solid for whatever time you want it rented and at your desired price? If you leave the renting to other hands, they may skim a fairly high percentage off the rent for their fee.

Say the mortgage and taxes at your new home come to $4,000 a year and you can rent the house at $4,000 a season. Will you be able to afford the other costs that go along with ownership, such as utilities, insurance, repair charges? Homes at the shore take a beating during the winter months, and your expenses for their exterior maintenance may be higher than for year-round homes inland. If you are many hours from that second home, it is important to have someone who lives there permanently check your property at least once a week when it is not in use, to see that winter blizzards or summer hurricanes have not caused damage, that the pipes have not frozen, a tree fallen, or any one of a few dozen other calamities befallen it. There may be costly telephone calls to workmen a hundred miles away. If you live in an area where it is possible, it would be wise to buy a house where the "season" is year-round, expanding your rental opportunities. Unfortunately, a beach house is one type property that does not lend itself to year-round renting, but homes in ski areas can afford attractive country living during the summer. These days some homes in Florida can be rented in the summer months.

Consider this too: It is difficult to be an absentee landlord when your primary home is many miles or a few states away from that vacation retreat. Who will notice if someone walks off with a couple of wicker chairs? Who will clean up between tenants?

A house inspection by a professional hired by you is important before buying any property; with a vacation home, it is vital. Some vacation homes conceal antiquated wiring, plumbing, and heating systems, if there is any heat at all.

Finally, it is best to look for a second home during the off-season. Everyone wants a beach house when the sun is shining and the ocean breezes cool the warmest day. But you will look far better to a seller in February, if the house has been on the market for a while. March to November are real estate brokers' busiest times, so if you can, shop in the other months.

Time-sharing Condominiums

The new concept in the condominium style of ownership called "time-sharing" has already been described. Here, instead of buying a condominium unit, you purchase the use of the unit for two weeks in August, say, or whatever time period you want, at a set price for twenty, thirty, or forty years. Time-sharing is popular in this country and abroad. There is a lengthier discussion of this vacation style in Chapter 4.

The Tax Picture

A second home brings the same tax advantages as a principal residence in that mortgage interest and property taxes are deductible. Some other benefits, however, have been reduced or scratched in new federal tax legislation, so if you think of that little bungalow as a total write-off, you will be wrong. The federal Tax Reform Act of 1976 closed several loopholes for second-home owners—for one, limiting the deductible visits an owner can make to "check" her property every year. The act also limits the deductions a homeowner can take if she uses a vacation home more than two weeks a year.

When you sell your principal residence, you can defer the capital-gains tax on any profit if you invest it in your next principal property within eighteen months. Vacation houses do not qualify for this exemption.

When You Sell

How you will fare when you want to sell a second home will depend on more vagaries than for a primary home. During a business recession, for instance, the market for second homes can dry up. And the investment value of this type of home is tied to its resale value.

Fortunately, most second-time owners do well at reselling time, thanks at least to inflation and the growing demand for this type of property. If you have extensively shaped up a run-down property in an excellent location, you will probably do very well indeed. But individual stories differ. Two New York couples got together and built a four-bedroom house in Vermont for $25,000 in 1970. They put in another $12,000 for various improvements. But they did not get up to Vermont as often as they thought they would, and they were not successful in renting the property either. They worried about it during those long, cold Vermont winters and finally decided to unload what had become more of a burden than a pleasure. So they sold it in 1976 for just $28,000. That case is an isolated one, but other sellers who stand, if not to lose money, at least not to make as reasonable a profit as they could otherwise expect, are those who own condominium units in overbuilt communities. Too many of such unsold units keep prices stagnant. Also, buyers might drift toward the newer models, rather than the resales. When you decide to sell, put the house on the market in the high season, when it and the area are most appealing. Buy in the off-season, sell in the high.

If buying a second home is at all in your plans, now is the time to act, just as the time will not be better than now to buy a primary home. You may be rewarded with a property you can enjoy now, and an investment that will grow with the passing seasons, high *and* off.

9

Living Together
and Protecting
Your Property Rights

If you have not already noticed, there is a new statistic that has been sneaking up on us: the number of couples living together out of wedlock has been rising steadily. According to the latest U. S. Census Bureau estimates, some 1.3 million unmarried persons shared living quarters in 1977, double the 1970 figure. They range from students bunking together in crowded off-campus apartments to retirees living in more luxurious accommodations.

Cohabitation, which is the legal term for living together, is still against the law in many states, although it is a law that is rarely enforced. After all, where would they put all the law-breakers? But the growing popularity of this style of living is bound to have an effect on existing law and the creation of new legislation to offer greater protection to both parties. The 1979 landmark case in California involving division of property between actor Lee Marvin and Michelle Triola Marvin (she legally changed her name to his), who had lived together for six years and then separated, had the California Supreme Court conceding "the mores of the society have indeed changed so radically in regard to cohabitation that we cannot impose a standard based on alleged moral considerations that have apparently been so widely abandoned by so many." Although Ms. Marvin, who claimed the actor had promised her lengthy support after their breakup, gained relatively little from the court settlement, considering the million-dollar-plus amount she had sought, the suit still promises to open the living-together arrangement to serious consideration by the state courts throughout the land.

If you are living with someone now, or are planning to, it would be wise for both of you to investigate your state's laws on cohabitation and the division of property if you should separate. There are many other points to consider in this arrangement, of course—alimony payments for divorced women who cohabit (forfeited in some states), the etiquette of the situation, splitting housekeeping chores, and so forth. But since this is a book about real estate, this chapter will concern itself only with the roof over the heads of the couple. Fortunately, that is a little more clearly defined than some of the other, newer, questions involved in cohabitation.

It is important for women to enter this relationship with a very clear idea of what they own now, what they intend to share, and what they are legally entitled to walk away with should the relationship end. Admittedly, this is not romantic. On the other hand, to shrug one's shoulders now can lead to years of bitterness later, after the arrangement ends and you are minus what you are entitled to and perhaps engaged in costly and emotionally draining legal battles. Remember, too, that while new legislation promises to protect both individuals, it is still up to those individuals right now to look after themselves. Women in living-together situations will probably never receive the legal protection that marriage offers. But the courts are trying to be fair. A written contract makes it easier for them to judge in a case. Oral promises are weak.

RENTING AN APARTMENT

The days of a landlord evicting an unmarried couple when the two names go on the mailbox are pretty much over. There are only a few states that make it a violation of the law to discriminate against an unmarried couple in rental housing, but even without that legislation, discrimination is fading. In states where that law is not in effect, of course, you *can* be refused an apartment. Discrimination does not cover an owner-occupied building of fewer than four units, providing the advertising isn't discriminatory. It depends on the landlord and frequently on the community. Arlene found that out when she and Tony moved into her four-room brownstone apartment in a small city with a heavy ethnic population. Her landlord, who lived in the building with his family, had actually complained to Arlene that she had too many "boyfriends." But Arlene felt her friends—male or female—were her own business and she went out of her way to avoid the landlord. When Tony moved in, the landlord, instead of being satisfied that Arlene was seeing only one man, as Arlene expected, instead blew up and evicted her. She did not want to pursue the matter in the courts, even if she had a case, because to return to the building would have been unpleasant. She and Tony moved to a medium-size apartment house a few blocks away where management did not care what their living arrangement was as long as someone's name was on the lease who could pay the rent.

This is the situation today. Large, impersonal apartment buildings usually do not care; apartments in private homes—well, it depends on the homeowners. You will probably be able to glance around your own neighborhood and know which buildings an unmarried couple should steer clear of.

If a man moved in with you and the lease is in your name, it does not matter what percentage of the rent he pays. Even if it is 100 per cent, you are responsible for the apartment. And legally you can make him move out if the relationship ends. If you move into his place, the reverse is true. If you go looking for a new place together, you will find as you read the lease carefully that most jointly signed leases provide that each signer is responsible for the entire rent. Be sure you can afford that total amount if you should ever have to carry it alone. If he moves out of your $500-a-month apartment, you have the legal right to sue him for his $250, but that can be time consuming and unpleasant. There are fine points here, too, which is another reason for having your housing decisions and wishes in writing. If, for instance, he moves out of his apartment and you stay and continue paying rent in his name, a court might find that you have assumed his landlord-tenant relationship.

Leases frequently say that only you or members of your immediate family can live in your apartment. Male/male and female/female roommates turn up all the time, of course, but cohabitation might have the landlord referring to this clause if he wants you out. If it should ever come to a court case, the judge is likely to rule in your favor, but still it is better not to sign a lease that limits your apartment to family members only.

It is also best not to lie about your relationship when apartment hunting. There are enough buildings that will accept you if a particular one does not. Sometimes couples will say they are engaged and the reluctant landlord rents them the apartment and nothing is said again about the matter. Sometimes, to avoid the hassle of apartment hunting, one party will merely move into the other's apartment. If you think that can work, it *is* a way around the whole brouhaha.

If you are moving to public housing you will be interested to know that in 1977 HUD added to its list of those eligible for public housing, unmarried couples or homosexual couples who "have evidenced a stable family relationship."

Once inside the apartment it is easy to avoid future disagreements by not making joint purchases. If one buys a rug, say, the other buys a chair. A house is somewhat different. Generally, both parties want to own it together.

BUYING A HOUSE

When buying a house, one of you can buy it in your own name or you both can buy it. When one party puts up all the money, lawyers recommend full legal ownership by that party. If you are both going to chip in, even if not in equal amounts, the question of title depends upon whether you want the right of survivorship. Joint tenants automatically inherit property from each other should the other partner die; tenants in common do not. The latter is more like a partnership, and you will be free to leave your share to whomever you designate in your will. If both names are on the deed and you later separate, you can sue, force sale of the property, and collect half the sale price. With real property—a house, a car—the property belongs to whoever holds title, courts say. With personal property—furniture, clothing—ownership is awarded to whoever paid for the items.

If you both own the house, the best way to handle ownership in the event of a breakup is to have a buy-sell agreement, which can be drawn up for you by your lawyer when you buy. That way, before the house is sold elsewhere, either co-owner has an opportunity to buy out the other person's share.

DISCRIMINATION BY LENDERS

A landlord may refuse to rent to unmarried couples and a seller may refuse them a house, but lending institutions are generally amenable to the relationship. Since the passage of the Equal Credit Opportunity Act of 1975, banks are no longer allowed to ask too many questions. They can ask if you are married, for example, but not to whom.

BUYING A CONDOMINIUM
OR COOPERATIVE UNIT

Unmarried couples have been purchasing condominiums together with no problem. Cooperatives are another matter, however. With the latter you have two potential problems. The owner may refuse to sell to cohabitors or the co-op board may refuse to approve the application. Your status should be mentioned to the realty agent before you begin shopping in order to avoid disappointment. In New York City, which has more cooperative buildings than any other city, the reaction to unmarrieds is mixed. Most couples there are renting and few try to buy apartments. Perhaps more would apply if they thought co-op boards would welcome them. Again, a real estate agent who works closely with cooperatives can give you the best indication of how the waters are where you live.

Couples who do buy a co-op usually put both names on the lease. Co-op boards prefer this as protection against what they feel is the inevitable split-up. Boards are more lenient toward couples who present themselves as engaged, and if one partner lives in the co-op alone and eventually a "roommate" moves in, the board tends to look the other way, as long as the couple makes no waves. As younger cooperators move into board positions, no doubt these rulings will ease.

COMMON LAW MARRIAGE

It has long been presumed that if a couple lives together for a set period of time—seven years is most often mentioned—the parties are automatically married, according to common law. This is the case in Alabama, Colorado, Georgia, Idaho, Iowa, Kansas, Montana, Ohio, Oklahoma, Pennsylvania, Rhode Island, South Carolina and Texas. If you move from a state that does recognize common-law marriage to one that does not, the latter will recognize that union. Before judging you married by common law, however, a court will look into many other details of your relationship besides your living together.

INSURANCE

If you and another party rent, your tenant's insurance policy can list both of you by name, even if only one of you signed the lease. Sometimes the second listing is for a "guest." You will pay more for the policy, which protects your possessions against theft and fire, than a married couple, but less than you would if you lived in two separate apartments. Be careful in your dealings with insurance companies, and in other areas as well for that matter, that you do not present yourselves as a married couple. That would constitute fraud, and in the case of insurance that could invalidate your policies.

A homeowner's insurance policy offers coverage for the house itself, its contents, and the homeowner's liability (an accident, say, where a visitor slips on your rug and decides to sue). The insurance company will almost always allow both your names on the section of the policy that covers the house itself, but just one name on the other two parts of the policy since you are not married. This coverage, too, can come a little higher than coverage for married couples.

Check around for the best rates, as you would for any purchase. Some companies put living togethers into a high-risk category, with correspondingly higher charges.

A CONTRACT

Cohabitors frequently draw up a contract for themselves outlining their respective duties and areas of ownership. It is in your best interest if the two of you have something in writing about your relationship. A written letter of agreement, notarized and stating whatever you want to say about the division of your property, is a document a court will try to honor. Oral promises are a hundred times more difficult to prove in court. A lease for an apartment is a contract and so is a deed to a house. Both outline ownership and liability. When you both buy a house, the lawyer you engage should be able to advise you what additional documents you will need for your mutual protection and will help you draw them up. Since in many states cohabitation is illegal, the courts are not likely to enforce a contract to engage in something illegal, but the times are changing fast in this area, with more and more concessions being made.

Some letters of agreement are binding. The enforcing of others is left to the discretion of the court. Those setting forth housekeeping duties, for example, have no legal status. Property contracts are enforceable, providing they are not based on what are called "meretricious," or sex-for-pay, relationships, so keep any mention of sex out of any document.

A WILL

Every working woman should have a will if any complication at all about the disposition of her estate could arise. And —don't laugh—you probably own more than you think you do. If you are single and want your property to pass on to your parents, you can probably do without a will because it would do just that since they are your next of kin and legal heirs if you die intestate. But even then having no will will lead to court delays and, too, it is likely there are special bequests you would like to make to other relatives and to friends. If you have bought a house with the man with whom you have been living and are joint tenants in the deed, he would inherit your half of the house in the event of your death. But if you are tenants in common, your share would go to your next of kin, unless specified otherwise in a will. No matter how young you both are, accidents happen. And if you are tenants in common and he has made no will, his half of the house you both love, and which he may have wanted you to have entirely, will belong to his next of kin. The average lawyer's charge for a will drawn up is $70. It is money well spent.

To sum up, the lease, the deed, the contract pertaining to joint residence—all carry more weight in court than oral promises and all the good intentions in the world. Unromantic as it sounds, get it in writing.

10

The Great Land Rush

There is something about being able to say "I've got some property downtown" or "We own land" that is irresistible. And that is partly why so many otherwise intelligent people make the blunders that lead them into purchasing worthless land. That and the desire for an investment that will pay off hundreds of times over when that land suddenly becomes valuable and a developer will (supposedly) pay anything for it. As the old saying goes, God stopped making land many years ago but he didn't stop making people. So all land is valuable, right? But there is land that is barren and rocky, land regularly hit by flash floods and miles and miles of desert land broiling under the sun. These, unfortunately, are some of the parcels that, sight unseen, uninformed buyers are paying out dollars for.

Investing in land is highly speculative, and developers' practices are riddled with deception and fraud. Most land does not rise in value simply because there is no demand for it. This country has vast open spaces for sale, but there is plenty of it that is not going to be used in the foreseeable future. So if you buy it, you will be holding on to it for a long time because no other buyer will want it.

Vacant land produces no income, yet you will have to pay property taxes on it every year, plus interest if you have financed the purchase. If you have paid cash, you will be losing interest on that money. If you decide to sell, the broker's commission here is a high 10 per cent. So that land had better grow in value for you to come out of a sale with a profit. Unless it doubles in value in seven years or so, you would have been better off putting your money into a high-yielding savings certificate or some other form of real estate investment.

That is not to say that some land purchases will not serve you well. Buying a little sliver of downtown in a city can return you triple your investment. A lakefront parcel with nothing working against it—environmental controls that will prohibit construction on that plot, for instance—should bring you a profit. But how can you tell good land from bad? Which parcel will take off and which will sit there, with only a few empty beer cans thrown its way, year after year after year? Aha, that's where the risk in investing comes in. Still, there are ways of lessening that risk by judicious studying of the market.

WHY INVEST ANYWAY?

If you are reading this book, you are probably looking for a home, not an investment in raw land—isn't that true? But, interestingly, after you have made that first purchase, you will probably want to buy something else. Your eye becomes trained to pick up the real estate advertisement in the newspapers. After looking at dozens of FOR SALE signs in front of suburban homes, you now notice them tacked onto office buildings or to trees in wooded patches outside town. A world of real estate opportunities you did not know existed has opened to you with the purchase of that house. And, eager little thing that you are, you want some of that property. You can see from house hunting how the prices of residential real estate have risen in the last few years. You want that to happen to you with a nonresidential investment. You will find that the purchase of a second piece of real estate will come about easier than the first.

One part of investing that will whet your interest is the tax-saving advantages. A tax shelter. Tax shelters are anything that protects your income from being taxed. Sheltering has always been thought of in terms of a haven for the ultrarich, but the gap between them and middle-income wage earners is narrowing as the latter find themselves in need of protection from *their* high tax bracket. Shelters are sought principally by those in the 50 per cent tax bracket, which means that that individual is at an income level where each additional dollar he earns is taxed at the rate of 50 per cent. But listen to this: That level is now $34,200 for single taxpayers and $47,200 for married persons.

Buying a home offers a tax shelter in that there are federal income tax deductions for mortgage interest and property taxes. An income-producing property also offers a sizable depreciation deduction, even though the property is, in fact, appreciating in value.

It is assumed that if you are thinking of investing, you are in a financial position to do so. You should have an adequate savings account—a few months of salary set aside for emergencies—and your insurance and pension contributions, if you are interested in the latter, provided for. Real estate investment is not "liquid." The money you put in you may not be able to get back easily and certainly not quickly. And, like all investments, it contains an element of risk, more in some ventures than in others. So this should be extra money, money to play around with, to start you on the way to becoming a real estate pro.

BUYING GOVERNMENT LAND

"Buy Cheap Government Land," "Free Government Land" scream the advertisements, and, indeed, who should be a better party to do business with than the U. S. of A.? Unfortunately, the advertisements are misleading. The government is no longer in the business of giving away land or even selling it inexpensively. The days of homesteading are over. Oh, there might be a free parcel once in a blue moon in the outreaches of Alaska, six hundred miles from the nearest community of any size, but that is it.

What the government does sell these days is land principally in the West. The tracts are relatively small—usually forty to a hundred acres, but sometimes larger than that, sometimes smaller. Many of these parcels are in barren country, far from public roads and utilities. There may be no access to the land at all; the government does not guarantee it. Land suitable for farming is rare, so there goes your vision of leading the simple life plowing the North 40. Most land is suitable only for grazing or mineral exploration.

The land is sold at auctions and there are somewhat fewer than a hundred of them held annually across the nation. Prices fetched are at or even a little higher than market value. Not cheap! You can submit a bid by mail, but if you want it to be competitive, you will, of course, have to attend the auction in person or send a representative. A certified check, money order, or cashier's check for a deposit or the total amount, whichever is required, must accompany a mailed bid.

For more information about buying government land, including periodic listings of what is available for sale, contact the Bureau of Land Management, U. S. Department of the Interior, Washington, D.C. 20240. The bureau has branch offices in Anchorage, Alaska; Boise, Idaho; Billings, Montana; Cheyenne, Wyoming; Denver, Colorado; Phoenix, Arizona; Portland, Oregon; Reno, Nevada; Sacramento, California; Salt Lake City, Utah; and Santa Fe, New Mexico.

Deal only with this agency. Far too many gullible would-be land buyers plunk down dollars for services and publications ("Cheap Government Land") that are produced by wheeler-dealers just for the suckers. Don't be taken in by those pitches.

The type of government land we are talking about here is not to be confused with "federal surplus lands," which were once used for government purposes but which are no longer needed. The most attractive surplus land parcels—recreational lands, islands—are usually passed on by the federal government to state and local agencies. But if you want to see what is available, contact the Regional Commissioner of the General Services Administration, Public Buildings Service, at a regional office in Atlanta, Georgia; Boston, Massachusetts; Chicago, Illinois; Denver, Colorado; Fort Worth or Houston, Texas; Kansas City, Missouri; Los Angeles, California; New York, New York; San Francisco, California; Seattle, Washington; or Washington, D.C.

BUYING LAND LOCALLY

The best real estate investing for the novice should be made within twenty-five miles of your home. There you will know the communities, the zoning ordinances, the population—its growth, income range, etc.—and the politics.

The most important factor in buying land is for you to be ahead of the crowd in anticipating where growth will occur. Naturally, you will be able to judge that better in your own backyard. When you have heard that land development has begun, you are already too late to buy at a reasonable or even bargain rate. The land is "hot."

Buy land that has the most potential uses. There is usually little that can be done with off-the-beaten-path swamp land unless you are holding out for pie-in-the-sky landfill. But land along a busy highway, which can be sold to a fast-food chain, gas station, or motel, can be a good buy. Land around a proposed shopping center, if you hear word of its construction before the masses, is good, too. Watch the zoning ordinances where you are looking. Land zoned for offices and stores generally has the best potential; then comes apartment buildings, industrial buildings, one-family homes, and farmland.

It will pay to keep an eye on what your state environmental

agency is planning to buy and where they will be putting a moratorium on development. A growing number of communities are attempting to slow over-all growth and lower speculation. No matter what use is suggested, they do not want it. "Land banks" are becoming more common. All of this could affect the resale of the acreage you buy.

If you are contemplating buying land, as in other areas of investment, the more people you talk to the more you will learn —and the more rumors you will pick up. Some of them you can profit by. When you get down to business, you will need a lawyer to go over every aspect of your purchase; a tax specialist, who is probably already handling your financial affairs; and a professional appraiser. The latter can give you the background of the land in which you are interested and its current value. And, of course, you will need a knowledgeable real estate broker.

What will grow on this land, if that is your intent? Do you plan to hold raw land for a long-term investment or do you want improved land? Do you intend to sell to the first buyer who makes a good offer, or are you considering plunking down a house on that plot one day? Remember, land is of no value without water or access. And what about sewerage? Electricity? Telephone? All of this should enter into your thinking about any lot you see.

Sophisticated buyers sometimes buy land auctioned by local authorities for the previous owner's nonpayment of taxes. If you try this, ask yourself these questions (after seeing the land, of course): Why did the owner abandon this land? Did he really not have the tax money or someone to pay that outstanding amount for him? Or is there something about the land itself that made it not worth holding on to? Perhaps it is too hilly or rocky to allow for construction of a house. Or there is no water in the area. As these properties are sold at auction, you can call the county tax collector and ask when the next auction will be held. When the list of properties to be sold is printed, they will send you one. You may have to visit the county assessor's or tax collector's offices to find out the assessed value of the property and if there are any liens on it. For the latter, you may have to visit the state's buildings department. You will have to do all the homework on these parcels yourself; there is no broker.

BUYING RESORT LAND

The number of free chicken dinners, with developers offering guests what is frequently turkey land, has diminished somewhat in the last few years because of tighter restrictions by the federal government. Land purchasing is still an area an investor should look at with extreme caution, however. Gullible people are still being talked into buying land sight unseen, principally in Florida, New Mexico, and Arizona, where more than two thousand land companies have opened for business in the last fifteen years. There are lots being offered in other states, too, where mountains, lakes, and other recreational facilities are the lures for buyers. Unprincipled developers look especially to eastern urbanites, who, they feel (and sometimes they are right), look at any vacant land as an outstanding investment opportunity and a chance to buy some of the country's few remaining open spaces.

The interstate land-sales industry is usually defined as comprising those companies engaged in selling subdivided land where the homes and other improvements on the site can be built and made at the expense of the buyer. You must seek out the best companies. They are not the ones that do the heaviest advertising, hustling free dinners and no-cost weekends at the site. Some of the largest advertisers in fact, are the ones offering the worst land.

The federal office of Interstate Land Sales Registration, which regulates those sales, has received as many as five thousand letters a year from people complaining of being swindled. Some thousand land development companies have been singled out by that agency for noncompliance with the Interstate Land Sales Full Disclosure Act when investigative teams went out to check for violations. These violations can take several forms: failure to meet deadlines for completion of facilities pledged in the offering statement; fabricated accounts of lot sales transmitted by radio to the salesperson who is driving the prospective buyer around the site; and, in one instance, lot sales were suspended when the developer was accused by HUD of failure to disclose certain information to prospective buyers, such as the fact that the subdivision "is in the immediate area of the ——— Lake Bombing Range"!

If you want to buy land in resort areas, whether for long-term investment or to build there eventually, consider these points:

▪ On-site inspection of the property is a must. If you see it, you might not buy it. No matter that a hustling salesperson guarantees you your money back in six months if you are not pleased, no matter how little the down payment is, *do not buy land sight unseen.*

▪ Before buying, check the subdivider's references. Reputable firms offering fifty or more unimproved lots must furnish you a set of government-required disclosure documents. You and your lawyer should go over them carefully. If you do not receive those documents at least forty-eight hours before you sign for the land, you can cancel the contract by notifying the seller by midnight of the third business day after you do receive them.

▪ Be sure you will be offered *clear title* to the property.

▪ When you make your on-site inspection of the land, do so in the worst season for that area. Go to Arizona in August. "It's hot as hell there then," said one resident. "It's up to around 115 degrees during the day and cools off to a 100 at night." Forget that old saw "It's a dry heat, with no humidity." It's still *very* hot. Palm Springs, California, on a 123-degree summer day is so hot you can't touch an outside doorknob without a cloth covering it. Land in Palm Springs is valuable no matter how baked its residents are in the summer because just now it is chic; new communities that land hustlers are selling are not. For more about retirees who moved to Florida, Arizona, and New Mexico, not necessarily to new subdivisions, and then moved back North, disillusioned, read the section "As You Approach Retirement" in Chapter 7, "Housing Choices for Special Times of Your Life." If you now live in a region with regular season changes, you may find the barren, burnt look of desert land a harsh shock.

■ Do not take promised amenities and developments for granted. If the developer promises shopping centers, golf courses, pools—well, he's under no obligation to provide them unless it is in writing in the contract. If you are going to build a house on your lot, that does not mean your neighbors will too. Yours may be the only home in a sea of vacant land.

■ *Can* the land be used as a homesite? What kind of permits must be obtained? Are there water and sewer hookups? What about access roads?

■ Also if you plan to build, consider where the financing for that house is to come from *before* you buy the land. Say you own land with water, electricity, and fire hydrants but no paved roads. A bank may turn you down for a mortgage just on the basis of the roads. If you shop around, you may find a lender, but how much easier to buy land where you know that when you want to build a house there, you can build a house there and no grief about it.

■ Sometimes a lot sale is made hundreds of miles from the subdivision headquarters. "But Mr. Smith, that lot is in the middle of no place. It's so far away from anything that I wouldn't want to be buried there." That was the cry of a Washington businesswoman who had finally viewed the Florida property for which she had been paying for over eight years. Another woman found the land she had bought was not big enough to build a house on under local zoning laws.

▪ Take the time to go home and think about your decision to buy. Don't be taken in by sales tactics that give you the impression there is only one lot left and if you don't buy it in the next half hour, you will be out of luck. Those fraudulent radio transmissions, for example. Have your lawyer *back home* look over all the printed material *first*. Do not engage a lawyer two blocks from the subdivision. Too many people in those locales are in the pocket of the developer.

▪ If the salesperson shows you that land prices in the development have risen over the last few years, it may be the company itself that is raising the prices, which hardly reflects the resale value of the land.

▪ Once you decide to buy, you will not, unless you pay in full, get title to the land or a mortgage. Instead, you sign a contract under which you agree to pay X dollars down and so much a month for as many as ten years. Interest ranges from 4 to 9 per cent. You do not get the right to build on that land until you have made all the payments.

▪ What will happen if you default on those payments? Be sure you understand how the company deals with payments and default. Most agreements give companies the right to take back the land and keep the money you have paid in. Sometimes you get back less than half the amount of the payments you have made. This is to absorb some of the developer's costs in advertising and parceling the land. It is better to expect very little in the way of a refund.

▪ If you already own subdivided land that you now want to sell, be wary of companies offering to do that for you for a fee of several hundred dollars in advance. Reputable developers offer sale programs, but they follow the usual practice of commissions paid *after* the sale is made. You should not have to pay anything in advance.

▪ Although there are tax depreciation deductions allowed with other forms of real estate investment, there is none with raw land because it is considered to have a limitless economic life.

The foregoing is quite a laundry list of "watch-out-fors" and "beware-ofs," but land-sale fraud is still quite a common occurrence. Be too clever to find that your patch of God's green earth is only a bit of ugly scrub. Educate yourself and then proceed with caution and a very healthy degree of cynicism about the claims you will hear.

11

Investing in Other Forms of Real Estate

There is more to real estate investing than buying raw land, and you can invest by yourself or with partners. Remember, though, that real estate investment, like any other investing program, carries a degree of risk, although knowledge of the market makes it a well calculated one. It is not a liquid investment either. Whatever you buy you may have to hold on to for years before you can sell. You cannot sell buildings, say, as quickly as art, jewelry, stocks, or bonds. Even when you find a buyer—and that can take time—it will take thirty or sixty days before closing, when you will get your money. You can borrow against the equity in the property you own, but even that will take a month before you get the cash in hand.

A quick run-through of what you are about to buy is not sufficient for wise investing. The property and the area of investment require constant surveillance. You must understand, too, the broader social forces that come to play on property values. Quite frankly, there are not that many men or women with the time or skill to devote to in-depth investing.

Try to read everything you can on your particular area of interest—apartment buildings, shopping centers, and so forth.

Talk to those who have purchased such properties. A report from the trenches means much more than theory. Take an evening adult education course in real estate investing, or attend any seminar offered by a local realty or mortgage office. Stay after class to get all your questions answered by the lecturer.

Look to the experts. Hire people to tell you what you do not know. You will need an accountant to advise you on your own financial picture and to go over the books of any property you intend to buy. You will need a lawyer to represent you throughout negotiations. Experts say it is better not to meet face to face with the seller. They say it is too easy for amateurs to give themselves away, either by words or with a look. Also by not meeting the seller you can avoid having him or her turn against you because of any bias he or she might have—in your case, because you are a woman perhaps. A good real estate broker can assist you in your hunt for investment property.

Don't take anyone's word for anything—the gross income of the building in which you are interested, the vacancy rate, the operating expenses, etc. See it all in writing. And let your team of experts see it. If the owner of the building says there are only two vacant apartments, drive around it on five successive evenings to see how many lights are lit. One man did that and found the place a tower of darkness. He passed up that purchase!

There is a saying in real estate that the three most important points to consider when buying are location, location, and location. You might add two others. First, never go into a deal that seems too good to be true. It wouldn't be offered to *you* if it were that good—the pros would have snatched it up. Second, it is best to stick close to home when you buy. It is not as glamorous as buying in another city or state, but you know your neighborhood better than any outsider, and conversely you will never know another one better than the one who is living there. Use that advantage and buy locally. Know the population of your community, its zoning ordinances, growth patterns, median income, schools, transportation. From all of that, you will be able to detect trends, which can lead to buying at a good price what will soon become "hot" and therefore unaffordable to the small investor. There is an element of luck that enters into successful investing. You may have to study and even hang around the right people in order to be able to take advantage of an opportunity the minute you spot it.

What follow are a few ways the amateur investor can take some first steps to a complex, fascinating, and potentially lucrative career as a real estate investor. When you have acquired experience, knowledge of the market, and a line of credit at your local bank, your mind will be brimming over with ideas for future projects, the next one always bigger than the last one. You will be a pro.

BUYING, FIXING UP, AND SELLING HOUSES

Buying, renovating, and selling houses, are increasingly popular enterprises for the small investor. It involves a low level of risk if you know where you are buying, which of course you will if you stick to a twenty-mile radius of where you live. It can yield a modest profit or, as you can read all the time from clever individual investor's success stories, a nice little fortune. Most buyers of this type of property remodel the house and then sell it quickly. Carrying a mortgage payment and taxes on the house for one day longer than necessary cuts back on profit. It is easier for two people to swing a career of doing this, for reasons that will become obvious, but a woman by herself *can* buy and remodel houses too. If she has a full-time job, the turnover rate of her property will be slower, however, than if there were two full-time people working on it. And naturally a slower turnover rate means a lower profit on that house.

Mary and Sam Weir, who are in their thirties, have purchased and renovated thirty-five homes on or near the New

Jersey shore, living in six of them along the way. Some have been run-of-the-mill beach houses, others thirty-five-room estates of historical and architectural significance. It became a full-time job for both of them, and led to their book, published in 1979, *How We Made a Million Dollars Recycling Great Old Houses*, Contemporary Books. $12.95.

Their first house cost $4,000 and it had been condemned. The couple worked on it, so much so that when they eventually moved out, they joked that the only original parts left were the roof beams. They turned the house into two apartment units—and they also managed to pay off the mortgage within six months. Sam worked for a chemical concern at the time; Mary was a housewife and new mother.

But here is where their fortunes took a turn different from the one most would have chosen—and why they are now millionaires-on-paper. Rather than sell that first house and move to a better one, in a typical upwardly mobile fashion, they held on to it and rented it. They bought another, larger house into which they moved and it cost $17,000. It took some scouring around for short-term loans to secure the down payment and trips to eight or nine banks for the mortgage commitment.

"After that, it became easier and easier," Mary recalled. "We could use equity in the houses for a down payment and only occasionally had to cough up cash. When we did, it came from rentals."

During the course of renovating house No. 2 and turning *it* into two apartments, Sam left his job with the chemical firm to concentrate on house recycling. He and Mary stayed in that house for three years and rented both apartments when they left. During those years they purchased three smaller houses.

A routine has now emerged. Sam does the plumbing and electrical work and has become an expert on the heating problems of old homes. Mary does most of the painting, papering, furniture repairing, and furnishing (some houses are rented furnished). She also handles the bookkeeping. But there is much overlapping of their jobs and no score is kept. Mary knows her way around a musty basement, too.

Recently, the couple divested themselves of half their holdings. The burden of carrying them had become too great and they are now eager to get into other areas, which almost always happens to small investors whose business grows like Topsy. But they originally rented the houses rather than selling them, first, to avoid paying capital-gains tax and, second, because properties in that shore area had risen in value even a few points higher than the prevailing average of from 10 to 13 per cent. Rents had risen too.

"Sure there's aggravation in renting," Mary says. "But tenants rarely call you if you fix things right the first time. It's nothing compared to the aggravation of a nine-to-five job.

"A large part of the work is getting started. And then just using common sense. After all, we've been around walls all our lives. So you make your best friends the paint and hardware stores.

"What it really is is making yourself go up that ladder every morning at 8 A.M., not putting it off. You can't diddle around all morning. Forget the ironing. Forget everything."

Mary and Sam, like other folks who are recycling houses, have enormous self-discipline. You have to *live* fixing up those houses. During Mary and Sam's early days—years, really—they and their two sons ate from paper plates. The boys helped cook—the littlest one was making his own oatmeal at five. The parents rarely watched television in the evening. There was the juggling of bills to worry about, too, in those days until things were on a more even keel. Many renovators are operating on the tightest of budgets. So if you want to become very rich from this type of investment, you will earn that money. It took Mary and Sam ten years—not long, really, for young people—but how many could lead a Spartan, work-filled, dog-tired life that long?

A word of caution for a prospective investor looking for these properties: Unless you can do almost all of the fixing up yourself, you will make little money on these ventures. If you must, call in professionals for only the most difficult tasks. The soundest way of buying is for you to find a house with good heating, plumbing, and electrical systems and in a decent neighborhood, but with no cosmetic appeal. Then put all your money and time into "charming it up"—paint, wallpaper, floor tiles, landscaping. Sometimes this will not take that much money at all but *will* take lots of imagination.

Mary and other renovators collect used furniture, antiques— anything that can be put to use eventually in the houses they buy. They haunt second-hand furniture stores, garage sales, auctions, and junkyards. All can yield moldings, mantels, shut- ters, lighting fixtures, stained-glass windows, and the like that can be incorporated into the house and bring a higher sale price. Pat, an interior designer who also is in the house resale business, imaginatively repainted a bed headboard and attached it to the lower half of the wall of a small dining "area" in one of her houses to give it more definition. She has just finished her third house—which brought her an 80 per cent profit but is admittedly in a community where houses are appreciating in value dramatically—and already has silent partners lined up waiting to put up the money for her next projects.

Besides buying a sound house in a basically good neigh- borhood, be sure that if the properties you buy are rental units, those rents can be raised to cover the money you have spent rehabilitating the house.

Before taking on an enormous project like this, ask yourself not only if you are capable of doing most of the work yourself, but also if you will have the time to devote to the house if you keep it and rent it. Will you have the patience to deal with tenants? Do you have extra cash for emergencies? What about credit? If you need it, can you get it?

BECOMING A LANDLADY

Suppose you do not want to sell and, like Mary and Sam, prefer to hang onto those houses you have remodeled. Or suppose you have purchased a home of your own with one or two rental units and are now a resident landlady.

Besides the tax advantages of deductible mortgage interest and property taxes, an income-producing property also offers deductions for depreciation, which can amount to quite a few dollars each year. (That deduction can be used even though the property has actually appreciated in fair market value.)

Ellen purchased a large modern house consisting of two floor-through apartments in a Boston suburb. She intended to occupy the top floor unit herself just as soon as the current tenant's lease expired. But her accountant pointed out that she would be able to obtain twice as much depreciation and tax shelter, as well as twice as much rent, if she didn't move in at all. So she now regards the property as purely an investment. The cash flow will be almost nonexistent for Ellen for a year or two until she can raise the rents on the two units. But the over-all appreciation of the house is there and so is her gradual buildup of equity.

But where does Ellen live herself? She and a friend rented an apartment at $275 a month. The income tax saving to her is greater than it would have been if she had lived in the house she owns.

Susan and her friend Herb also bought a house that neither plans to live in. It is a single-family home costing $41,700 in a rapidly appreciating suburban community. Each put up half the down payment. They intend to do some rehab work, then lease the house for enough money to cover mortgage and property taxes.

Susan says her application for a mortgage was accepted even though she was earning no more than $12,000 that year as a

legal librarian. But the home in which she had been living she
had inherited from her parents, free and clear. The ease with
which she secured the financing she attributed to the equity in
that house. But then she added that the loan officer became
very attentive when Susan mentioned that she had been studying the fine points of the Equal Credit Opportunity Act
as part of her work at a nearby university for a real estate
salesperson's license. In a light tone and smiling a little, Susan
inquired of the officer if it was true that the lender, if brought
to suit for violation of the ECOA, could be liable for punitive
damages of $10,000 in individual actions and up to $500,000,
or 1 per cent of its net worth, whichever is less, in class ac-
tions? She received her mortgage commitment letter two
weeks later, a record for that particular lending institution, the
real estate agent remarked.

If you now own a house, give serious thought to hanging on
to it and renting it rather than selling if you want to move. Of
course, if you inherit Great-aunt Tillie's home three states
away, it would probably be better to sell. But if you own a
home and want to move to an apartment or if you are getting
married and you both want to buy a new place, try to rustle up
the money to buy the new house without selling the one you
have now. Remember, houses are rising in value around 12 per
cent right now. If you sell and deposit your profits in a bank—a
foolish move—you will be getting yearly bank interest of half
that.

Renting brings it own aggravations, of course, and you must
be aware of the problems you will encounter and able to cope
with them. One of the greatest, property owners say, is rent
control, which in many communities in many states keeps rents
from being raised more than from 5 to 7 per cent a year.
Owners say that small amount does not nearly cover the rising
costs of fuel, labor, taxes, and other running expenses. Naturally, this is more of a problem in multiunit buildings than in
private houses with one or two small units.

Ellen and Susan expect the rents they collect from their

houses to cover mortgage and property taxes and they're probably right. But rents do not often totally cover other expenses, such as fuel, insurance, and the repairs that are called for on any property. Some of these can be major expenses. Some are tax deductible, yes, but you still have to make that cash outlay.

If homeowners who are landlords in their own houses have their problems, the owners of apartment buildings—well, some of them find it so difficult to survive they simply turn the key on their buildings and walk away. And that is how slums are born—have you seen pictures of all those vacant buildings in the South Bronx, in New York City? There are real estate brokers in some areas who say flatly that anyone buying a six-to-ten-unit-apartment building from them is a fool. Well, perhaps those buyers have just not done their homework. Many building owners claim the structure must have at least nineteen units if there is to be money left over after you have paid your running expenses. In buildings of six or more units, you will need a first-class manager living on the premises to oversee things for you. If you think you can take over a derelict building in a rundown location, remember those pictures of the South Bronx. Many socioeconomic forces combined to produce such devastation: rent controls, a shifting population, increasing number of tenants on welfare, and rising operating expenses.

In buying a multifamily dwelling, a house inspection by a professional is *vital*. The inspection report will tell you, down to the minutest detail, just what ails that building. Also, be sure to have written into any purchase offer you make for the property that the sale is contingent not only on a favorable inspection and other common points, but also on approval of the seller's federal income tax returns for that property for the two preceding years. The returns will not lie—or they should not—about income for that building. If you want the small apartment house you buy delivered vacant, so that you can do substantial renovation, that should be written into the purchase contract as well. Sometimes it works, sometimes it doesn't.

An apartment house that contains mostly one-bedroom units

is the best investment. Efficiency apartments attract transients and the turnover rate is high; two- and three-bedroom units are more difficult to rent. A vacancy rate of from 5 to 8 per cent of gross annual income is acceptable. It has often been said that a buyer of such properties should expect to pay seven times the annual gross rental income, but what is far more important is the *net* income in these days of rising maintenance and repair costs.

COMMERCIAL PROPERTIES

If the idea of being a landlady in residential properties does not appeal, consider commercial real estate. Not that many amateur investors do think of that area immediately. Yet it can bring a lot less aggravation than managing apartment units. A commercial property—store, factory, office building, warehouse, parking lot—will not give you tenants calling about no water at 2 A.M. Usually there is no one (except perhaps a security guard) in those building from about 7 P.M. until 7 A.M. the following day. There are no rent controls here. Maintenance costs can frequently be tied into rents. Leases are long—twenty years or more. Tenants will be reputable—you will check their credit rating before leasing to them. We are not talking about forty-story office buildings here. But there are excellent buys in 5,000–6,000-square-foot buildings, costing from $50,000 to $60,000, perhaps in your own neighborhood. They may be occupied by doctors or lawyers or other professionals. Investment profits can be quite good here. Owners of some properties can earn as much as 25 per cent of invested capital, although more likely it is closer to 8 or 9 per cent. Look for at least 10 per cent. You can exercise considerable leverage here since down-payment requirements may be low if the lender believes the property has a good income potential.

Look, too, for rundown properties in revival neighborhoods, as one successful woman investor did. Or, if you are more conservative, stick to the business section of town. Besides existing office buildings, factories, etc., look at unique buildings with an eye toward other uses than what they were constructed for. There is a silo in New Jersey, for instance, that now contains offices; huge Victorian houses have become doctors' offices or headquarters for professional societies; unused railroad depots have become first-class restaurants. Keep an eye on what the needs of the community are likely to be—then step in with the perfect idea.

Many amateur investors cling to the reaction of the home-owner when they first see commercial investment proper-ties: it is the wrong color, it is an ugly building, *I* wouldn't want to live there. Well, you *aren't* going to live there, so don't let this kind of thinking get in the way of your purchasing a good property. In fact, if there is something hideous about the parcel—it is an unimaginative chunk of concrete or is painted chartreuse—that may turn off other buyers, you, in your sophis-tication and ability to see beyond unimportant details, may get yourself quite a buy. And after all, what does a paint job cost? $1,000? In general, the purchase price should not exceed 100 times the *gross* monthly rent.

A LITTLE HELP FROM YOUR FRIENDS

If you have a few thousand dollars but not quite enough to purchase any property, why not join with a few female friends in investing? If you form a partnership, you will be able to buy *now*.

If you are pooling money with others, there must be a very strong contract defining the method of taking title, how rents are to be collected, which of you is to pay the real estate taxes, what will happen if the property is to be sold, and what hap-pens if a member defaults in her mortgage payment.

A group banding together like this will usually form a "lim-ited partnership." Each limited partner contributes her share of the down payment and monthly mortgage payment and receives, in turn, her share of the cash flow and tax deductions. Limited partnerships must have a "general partner," who is usually the person who organizes or manages the property—collects the rents, pays the taxes, hires the building superintendent, etc. The limited partners then have no day-to-day involvement with the property.

Look for women to join you who are approximately your age and share your goals. Four women in their twenties and thirties may be willing to hold onto a building for many years, while four women in their fifties, perhaps anticipating retirement and subsequently reduced incomes, may want to buy in a rapidly appreciating neighborhood and sell at a handsome profit after four or five years. Remember, however you buy, that there is, as in just about all forms of real estate investment, no liquidity here.

SYNDICATES

"Syndication" is taking that partnership of a few friends a few notches higher, to where the really high rollers are. The Empire State Building, in New York City, for instance, is owned by a syndicate. Most buildings that size are nowadays owned by institutional investors and pension funds, but smaller properties are still syndicated or owned by individuals. Most of the members of a syndicate are usually lawyers, accountants, and real estate brokers who are involved with the buildings in some manner. These are sophisticated investors in the 50 per cent or higher tax bracket and they are looking for tax shelters and not immediate income. Syndicates are usually *private* partnerships that do not look for outside investors.

Public syndication offerings, however, frequently look for taxpayers in brackets lower than the 50 per cent one to invest. Many of these buyers are said to be those with $45,000 or so of taxable income, filing joint returns. The amounts of their investment can be as low as $3,000. Some public syndicates diversify their holdings, buying motels, department stores, factories, and commercial and industrial buildings. Since all public offerings must be registered with the federal Securities and Exchange Commission (SEC), a complex prospectus is available to buyers, so you will have plenty to read before you plunge in.

In "blind pool syndicates" there is no commitment by the general manager to purchase any particular type property. The manager may invest wherever he or she thinks is wise, unless prohibited by the syndicate agreement. (This can also be called a "nonspecified syndicate.") Some have realized rates of 15 per cent or higher—certain purchases under the Empire State syndicate are understood to be paying their limited partners annual returns as high as 22 per cent—but a return lower than that figure is more likely.

Among the major public real estate funds are JMB Realty Corporation of Chicago, Illinois; the Robert A. McNeill Corporation of San Mateo, California; Integrated Resources of New York, New York; and the Fox & Carskadon Financial Corporation of Palo Alto, California.

If you have neither the time nor inclination to look after your realty investments, perhaps syndication is for you.

Syndicates and real estate investment trusts (REITs) ran into hard times a few years back because of a number of economic and organizational factors. In the case of REITs (pronounced "REETS"), which were the favored means of investing in real estate five or six years ago, the principal problems were growing too fast and too much borrowing to acquire more assets. The trend is now back to syndicates, which were favored before REITs. REITs are still chancy for the first-time investor whose every dollar must count.

This chapter and the preceding one are an introduction to the areas of real estate investment that you as an amateur might consider. They are designed to whet your interest. Read all you can on these kinds of investment. There is not necessarily good and bad advice—there is just advice that differs according to the writer or speaker. It is speculation, and there are many opinions on how to get rich. One of the classics in real estate investment is *How I Turned $1,000 into $3 Million in Real Estate in My Spare Time*, revised edition, by William Nickerson (Simon and Schuster, 1969, $8.95). Making a bundle can be done even today. But it takes keen knowledge, total absorption, plenty of hard work, and a little luck! Maybe several years, too. But the rewards can be great. And it *is* fun. Go to it.

12

Quick-Reference
Glossary
of Realty Terms

ABANDONED BUILDING A structure, usually a multifamily dwelling, that has been given up by a landlord who considers his investment lost and has no intention of reclaiming his property.

ABSTRACT OF TITLE The summary of the history of the legal title to a piece of property.

ACCELERATION CLAUSE The requirement that the entire balance owed on a loan be paid when one or two payments are overdue.

AIR RIGHTS The title, vested in the owner of a parcel of land, to the use of the air space above the land. Frequently granted for the space above railroad tracks, highways, etc. Probably the most notable use of air rights is Madison Square Garden, in New York City, which was constructed over Conrail's Pennsylvania Station.

AMENITIES Features of a property that make it more salable to buyer or renter—pool, clubhouse, and the like.

AMORTIZATION The prorated repayment of a debt. Your mortgage is being amortized every month that you make payment to the lender.

APARTMENT, GARDEN   An urban unit with the entrance on the ground floor and the use of a back- or frontyard. May also refer to a two-story complex usually in a suburban setting.

APARTMENT, RAILROAD   Indigenous to older urban buildings, these units are laid out so that one room follows another, railroad-car style.

APPRAISAL   The procedure employed by professional appraisers hired by you to estimate the value of a piece of property.

APPURTENANCES   Whatever is annexed to land or used with it that will pass with the conveyance of title—e.g., a garage, a gatehouse.

ASSESSED VALUATION   The value placed on land and buildings by a government agency for tax purposes, usually a percentage of market value.

ASSESSMENT   The tax levied on property by a taxing authority to pay for certain new improvements.

BINDER   An advance agreement between buyer and seller to purchase property, subject to certain conditions. Usually accompanied by a sum of money smaller than the down payment.

BLOCKBUSTING   The unlawful practice employed by some realty brokers of increasing the selling of houses in a neighborhood by circulating rumors that numbers of minority people are moving in and will lower existing property values. The blockbuster's objective is to see sale prices drop substantially in the subsequent panic selling. The broker then sells the house at inflated prices to minority families. Blockbusting can lead to the loss of the culpable broker's license.

BUFFER ZONE   An area that separates two or more types of land use from each other.

BUILDER'S WARRANTY   The written statement by a builder guaranteeing that a building was completed in conformity with a stipulated set of plans and specifications. Its purpose is to protect the purchaser from latent defects in the building. The warranty can last up to ten years.

BUILDING CODE   The state or locally adopted regulation, enforceable by police powers, that controls the design, construction, repair, quality of building materials, use, and occupancy of any structure in a specific locale.

CARRYING CHARGES   For homeowners, these comprise mortgage and interest payments, real estate taxes, and other running costs of ownership. In condominiums and cooperatives they comprise the monthly maintenance charge that pays for major repairs to the complex, upkeep of the common areas, insurance, employee salaries, and so on.

CERTIFICATE OF OCCUPANCY   Known as a "C of O," this is the resident's official authorization to occupy premises. It states that the use and conditions of a new or rehabilitated building are consistent with the zoning ordinances of the locality.

CHATTELS   Articles of personal property such as household goods and furnishings.

CLOSING COSTS   One-time charges payable at the actual transaction where property passes from one owner to another. Includes charges for title search and insurance, attorney's fee, property survey, mortgage application fee, and points (see Points below), where charged. Also known as "settlement costs."

COHABITATION   The legal term for "living together."

COMMON FACILITIES   Areas in a condominium, cooperative, or mobile-home community shared by all residents; these include hallways, grounds, laundry room, and recreational facilities.

COMMUNITY ASSOCIATION   The group of joint owners of a condominium or townhouse community that governs the community.

CONDOMINIUM   The housing style where the buyers own their apartment units outright, plus an undivided share in the common facilities of the community.

COOPERATIVE The housing style where buyers purchase shares in the corporation that owns the building and holds the mortgage on it. The number of shares varies according to the size of the apartment unit and its purchase price. Tenant-shareholders have a proprietary lease that gives them the right to their units.

DEED The legal document that conveys to a person or persons the title to real property.

DEFAULT The failure of a homeowner to meet certain contractual obligations, such as a mortgage payment. Default can lead to foreclosure (*see below*).

DENSITY The number of dwellings and commercial units per acre of land. Can also refer to people—e.g., ten people per acre.

DEPRECIATION The gradual loss in the value of buildings and fixtures (but not land) over a period of time, excluding accidents. A tax depreciation allowance is granted to owners of income-producing property.

DWELLINGS, MULTIPLE Buildings comprising three or more living units having common access.

EARNEST MONEY The sum paid as a binder on a contract of sale.

EASEMENT RIGHTS The rights of one person to use of land owned by another, such as a common driveway, access road, etc. Water, sewerage, and utility suppliers frequently have easement rights across property.

EMINENT DOMAIN The right by which a government may acquire private property for public use without the consent of the owner, but upon payment of reasonable compensation.

ENCROACHMENT The extension of a building onto the land of another.

EQUALIZED ASSESSED VALUATION The value placed on real property for tax purposes by a local government, as corrected to approximate market value.

EQUITY   The value of a property exclusive of its mortgage and other liens upon it. Equity increases with each mortgage payment.

ESCROW   Money or a deed placed in the keeping of a third party until obligations by the other two sides, set out in the escrow agreement, have been fulfilled.

EXCLUSIONARY ZONING   The abuse of zoning laws to exclude low-income groups from desirable residential areas. Many court cases against suburban communities have come up in the last few years charging that zoning laws are creating economic and racial segregation.

EXCLUSIVE AGENT   One real estate broker with the exclusive right to sell a particular property within a specified period of time. The property becomes an "exclusive listing."

EXURBIA   The semi-rural area just beyond the suburbs.

FHA   The Federal Housing Administration, an agency created within HUD (*see below*) to insure mortgages on residential property. These mortgages are offered to home buyers usually at a fraction of a percentage point less than the prevailing commercial rate and with lower downpayment requirements.

FmHA   The Farmers Home Administration, an agency in the Department of Agriculture that insures home loans in communities of less than 10,000 population.

FORECLOSURE   Legal proceedings instigated by a lender to deprive a person of ownership rights when mortgage payments have not been kept up.

GROUPERS   A number of persons, usually single, who band together to rent an apartment or house. Groupers are most often found in resort areas and college towns, and their presence has, in recent years, led to zoning ordinances in some communities prohibiting the use of houses by unrelated persons.

HOLDOUT   A property owner who refuses to sell, thus preventing the assemblage of a site from being completed.

HOUSING AUTHORITY   A local public body empowered to provide and manage housing, especially for low-income groups and the elderly. Housing authorities aim to clear slums, issue bonds, and in general carry out the public housing program of a town or city. All depend on federal subsidies, though a few also operate with state or municipal funds.

HOUSING CODE   The local regulations setting forth minimum conditions under which dwellings are considered fit for human habitation. Intended as a safeguard against unsanitary or unsafe conditions and overcrowding.

HUD   The United States Department of Housing and Urban Development, from which the federal government's housing programs flow, excluding FmHA programs.

"IN REM" FORECLOSURE   The legal action of local authorities to take property ownership from a person who has not paid taxes for a specified period of time. The city or local taxing authority then becomes owner of the property and frequently disposes of it by auction.

INDUSTRIAL PARK   An area ranging from a few hundred to several thousand acres zoned for industrial uses, usually with common services for tenants. Many comprise low-rise buildings in suburban or exurban parklike settings.

INFRASTRUCTURE   The basic equipment, utilities, installations, and services necessary for running a city. Includes roads, bridges, railways, public transportation, and, on the larger scale, the nation's military installations.

LAND BANK   An accumulation of vacant land by a municipality for future use not yet determined.

LAND, RAW   Any land available for building, but lacking utilities or improvements.

LAND-USE PLAN   The official formulation by a community of how it will use its land in future years—e.g., for residential, commercial, industrial, or institutional purposes.

LEVERAGE   The employment of a small investment to generate a greater rate of return through borrowing. Employed by as-

tute investors, the most common form of leverage is homeowners' using a small down payment to purchase a house,
obtaining the largest mortgage possible. In other words, buy
as much as you can, with as little outlay of cash as possible.

LIEN   A claim recorded against a property as security for payment of a debt. If the lien is not removed or the debt is not
cancelled, the property may be sold to satisfy the holder of
the lien.

LIFE CARE FACILITY   The housing style where a buyer purchases an apartment unit, plus total medical services, for the
duration of her life for a flat purchase price and then pays
monthly maintenance charges thereafter. In true life care facilities, buyers pay all costs except those ordinarily picked
up by Medicaid.

LOFT   A structure of more than one story that was built originally for storage, manufacturing, or some other commercial
use. Now often used for residential purposes (frequently illegally).

"LOW BALLING"   A practice of builders of underestimating carrying charges in a new condominium or townhouse project
to make the development more attractive to buyers. The
builder initially absorbs any extra costs himself; then, when
the community is completed and control is passed on to the
residents, they are hit with more realistic, and much higher,
monthly maintenance costs.

MANUFACTURED HOUSING   Homes that are built piecemeal in a
factory, with components shipped to the building site where
they are then assembled.

MORTGAGE, BALLOON   A loan where borrower pays all or
mostly all of just the interest until the end of the loan when
the principal becomes due. At that time the lender will often
refinance the loan, frequently at a higher rate of interest.

MORTGAGE, CONVENTIONAL   The form of mortgage most popular with lenders, not guaranteed by the FHA or VA (*see
below*), and thus with no restriction on the rate of interest.

MORTGAGE, GRADUATED   A loan where the borrower's payments rise over the length of the mortgage, on the general assumption that the borrower's income is rising too.

MORTGAGE, OPEN-END   A loan with a provision that permits the borrowing of additional money in the future over an extended amortization period.

MORTGAGE, SECOND   A lien on property beyond the original mortgage. Since this "junior mortgage" offers the lender less security than a first mortgage—the first must be *paid* first—it usually calls for a higher interest rate and a shorter repayment period.

MORTGAGE, VARIABLE-RATE   A loan where the rate of interest fluctuates over the course of the mortgage according to several agreed-upon economic factors.

MORTGAGEE   The lender (bank or other institution) to whom the property is mortgaged.

MORTGAGOR   The borrower under a mortgage.

MULTIPLE LISTING SERVICE   An organization that compiles a list of houses and other properties for sale that is distributed periodically to subscribing area real estate brokers.

NET LEASES   In commercial properties, a stipulation in the lease that the tenant pays all insurance, taxes, utility, and repair bills. Usually the rent is lower, but this arrangement frees the owner from all expenses save for the upkeep of the building's exterior and his or her own mortgage payments.

OPTION   The exclusive right of a person to purchase or lease a property at a stipulated price or rent within a specified period of time.

PERCENTAGE LEASES   Leases enabling landlords to collect from retail stores either a flat rent or a percentage of the business's gross sales, whichever is larger.

PLANNED UNIT DEVELOPMENT (PUD)   A residential complex of mixed housing types. Offers greater design flexibility than traditional developments, which means frequent economic advantages. PUDs permit clustering of houses, sometimes not allowed under standard zoning ordinances, utilization of open space, and projects harmonious with the natural topography.

POINTS   A one-time fee that the lender charges buyer or seller in granting a mortgage. Lenders charge points when making a loan that might not otherwise be granted because of local economic conditions, location of the property, and so forth. One point is 1 per cent of the amount of the mortgage. Payment is due at closing.

PUBLIC DOMAIN   Land owned by the federal government.

PUBLIC HEARING   A meeting, open to everyone, that is required by law before land may be acquired for a project that requires public funding. Provides an opportunity for private citizens and community organizations to present their views on the proposal.

PROSPECTUS   The document offered by a condominium or co-operative sponsor detailing ownership of the development, prices, and layouts of the units, procedures for purchase, and numerous other aspects of how the project will be sold and run.

REDLINING   The alleged practice of some lending and insurance institutions involving their refusal to make loans or to issue insurance policies on properties they deem to be bad risks.

RENT CONTROL   The regulation by a local government agency of rental charges, usually according to set formulas for increases.

RIPARIAN RIGHTS   The right of a property owner whose land abuts a body of water to swim in that water, build a wharf, etc.

SCATTER-SITE HOUSING   Multifamily dwellings dispersed in small numbers throughout a middle-income community by a local housing authority to achieve economic and/or racial integration.

SEMIDETACHED HOUSE   One structure containing two dwelling units separated vertically by a common wall.

SETTLEMENT COSTS   *See* Closing costs.

SQUATTER   One who occupies another's property illegally.

STATUTORY TENANT   A renter whose lease has expired, but who is still protected by its provisions.

SURVEY   An exact determination by a surveyor of just where an owner's property begins and ends.

TENANTS IN COMMON   Parties who have a property-purchase arrangement whereby joint owners do not have any automatic right of survivorship; each leaves his or her share of the property to whoever is designated in his or her will.

TENANTS, JOINT   Parties who have a property-purchase arrangement whereby joint owners automatically inherit another's share upon death. Property purchased by married couples is usually in this style.

TIME SHARING   A plan whereby a condominium shopper can purchase a percentage of a furnished unit based on the time period she wants to live in it—one or two weeks a year or longer—at a set price, for twenty, thirty, or more years. Usually found in resort areas.

TITLE   Evidence, usually in the form of a deed, that a person is the legal owner of the property in question.

TITLE INSURANCE   A contract whereby a title insurance company guarantees to make good to a homeowner a property's loss that could be incurred from defects in a title.

TITLE SEARCH   A detailed investigation to assure that property is being bought from the legal owner and that there are no liens or special assessments against it. Mortgagees frequently require both title search and insurance.

TOWNHOUSE   A two- or three-story city row house usually of some architectural merit and usually high price, or an apartment complex operating under the condominium form of ownership.

URBAN RENEWAL   The renovation or restoration of a section of a city—e.g., demolishing slums, rehabilitating housing, building up the commercial center, providing more and better amenities.

VACANCY RATE   The ratio between the number of vacant apartment units and the total number of units either in a specific building or in an entire city. When the vacancy rate in a city falls below 3 to 5 per cent, that usually means a housing crisis for would-be renters. The precise figure is difficult to determine, however, because some urban units are considered no longer habitable and vacancies checked with utilities and telephone companies fluctuate.

VARIANCE   A specially granted departure from prescribed zoning requirements—e.g. a variance would be needed to open a boutique in the ground floor of one's home if that block were zoned for residential use only.

VA   The Veterans Administration. An independent federal agency that operates a loan-guarantee program for honorably discharged veterans and widows of men who died of service-related injuries. Low or sometimes no down payments are required, the interest rate is slightly below the prevailing commercial figure, and no points are charged qualified borrowers.

ZONING   The procedure whereby a locality classifies real property for a number of different specified uses—residential commercial, industrial, etc.—in accordance with a land-use plan. Ordinances are enforced by the governing body of a locality.

Index

Ruth Rejnis, formerly on the news staff of the New York *Times*, has written for *New York*, *Family Circle*, *Reader's Digest*, *Apartment Life*, and other magazines in the area of housing and real estate. She is the author of *Everything Tenants Need to Know to Get Their Money's Worth* and *A Woman's Guide to New Careers in Real Estate*.

Ms. Rejnis lives in Hoboken, N.J., where she has just begun her own real estate investment career with the purchase of an income-producing brownstone.